RELIGIOUS EXPERIENCE AND RELIGIOUS BELIEF

Essays in the
Epistemology of
Religion

Edited by

Joseph Runzo
Craig K. Ihara

UNIVERSITY
PRESS OF
AMERICA

LANHAM • NEW YORK • LONDON

Contributors

Alvin Plantinga
Kai Nielsen
William P. Alston
David J. Kalupahana
Nelson Pike
John Hick
Joseph Runzo

Copyright © 1986 by

University Press of America,® Inc.

4720 Boston Way
Lanham, MD 20706

3 Henrietta Street
London WC2E 8LU England

Library of Congress Cataloging in Publication Data

Religious experience and religious belief.

"The basis for this volume of essays is the
Eleventh Annual Philosophy Symposium at California State
University, Fullerton [in 1981] on 'religion,

mysticism, and knowledge' "—Acknowledgements.
   Bibliography: p.
   1. Knowledge, Theory of (Religion)—Congresses.
2. Religion—Philosophy—Congresses.   3. Experience
(Religion)—Congresses.   I. Runzo, Joseph, 1948-
II. Ihara, Craig K., 1943-   .   III. Plantinga, Alvin.
IV. Philosophy Symposium (California State University,
Fullerton).   (11th : 1981 : California State University,
Fullerton)
BL51.R353   1986   291.4'2'01   86-1614
ISBN 0-8191-5292-7 (alk. paper)
ISBN 0-8191-5293-5 (pbk. : alk. paper)

Cover design by Anne Masters

All University Press of America books are produced on acid-free
paper which exceeds the minimum standards set by the National
Historical Publications and Records Commission.

For my wife, Claire; my mother, Grace;
    and my grandmother, Ito.

                    Craig K. Ihara

        For my loving parents,
    Joseph V. and Ruth O. Runzo

                    Joseph Runzo

Contents

Acknowledgements

The basis for this volume of essays is the Eleventh Annual Philosophy Symposium at California State University, Fullerton, on "Religion, Mysticism and Knowledge." Our first thanks go to those who made that symposium possible. In addition to the seven primary speakers, whose revised papers are included in this volume, the faculty and students who served on the Symposium Committee deserve a large measure of credit. Faculty on the committee included Peter Dill, Gloria D. Rock, Betty Safford, Frank Verges, and David J. Depew. Students who made major contributions in symposium planning and/or served as commentators on student panels were David Barlow, Vickie Cafferky, Roberto Elizondo, Lauren Jensen, Richard A. Kasa, Charles S. Kinzie, and Bronson Pittman. In addition, Dr. Ronald Burr commented on the paper by David Kalupahana.

Dean Don Schweitzer of C.S.U.F. deserves special thanks for his important support for the symposium. Mrs. Elaine Weidner and her staff, including Sonia Rehnborg, Wilma Lazar, and Billie Smith at C.S.U.F, facilitated both all phases of the symposium and several steps in the publication of this volume.

For the symposium, major financial support was provided by the C.S.U.F. Departmental Associations Council. Other funding came from the Philosophy Club, the Office of the President, the School of Humanities and Social Sciences, and the Philosophy Faculty, all of California State University, Fullerton. An additional contribution was made by Mr. Mark Klein.

For the book, Chapman College generously provided the word processing and typesetting services for the preparation of the manuscript. Here special thanks go to Debra Hughes, Chapman Philosophy Department Secretary; Sidney West, Director of the Computer Center; Judy Mora, Word Processing Coordinator; and Annie Long, Director of Publications. Funds for proofreading and other incidental expenses came from the C.S.U.F. Office of Faculty Research. Diane and Gordon Brown of Textperts provided invaluable proofreading for the entire manuscript.

Finally, we are especially grateful for the support and help which our wives, Claire and Jean, gave us during the preparation of this volume.

Craig K. Ihara and Joseph Runzo

Contributors

WILLIAM P. ALSTON (Ph.D., University of Chicago) has published extensively in the philosophy of religion, philosophy of language, epistemology, philosophy of mind, and the philosophy of psychology. He has published four books, including Philosophy of Language and Religious Belief and Philosophical Thought: Readings in the Philosophy of Religion, and contributed eighteen articles to the Encylopedia of Philosophy. Alston has served as President of the American Philosophical Association, Western Division; the Society of Christian Philosophers; and the Society for Philosophy and Psychology. He has taught at the University of Michigan; Rutgers University; the University of Illinois, Urbana-Champaign; and is currently Professor of Philosophy at Syracuse University.

JOHN HICK (D. Litt., Edinburgh; D. Phil., Oxford; Ph.D., Cambridge) has published many articles in the philosophy of religion and in theology, and is the author of nine books and the editor of seven others. His publications include Faith and Knowledge, Philosophy of Religion, Evil and the God of Love, Death and Eternal Life, God and the Universe of Faiths, and Problems of Religious Pluralism. He has taught at Cornell University, Princeton Theological Seminary, Cambridge University, and the University of Birmingham (U.K.). Hick is currently Danforth Professor of the Philosophy of Religion at Claremont Graduate School.

CRAIG K. IHARA (Ph.D., University of California, Los Angeles) works in the fields of Oriental philosophy and ethics. His published articles have appeared in such journals as Ethics and Philosophical Topics, and he is a contributor to Masterpieces of World Philosophy. He is currently Professor of Philosophy and Chairperson of the Department of Philosophy at California State University, Fullerton.

DAVID J. KALUPAHANA (Ph.D., University of London) has published numerous articles on Buddhism and is the author of eleven major and thirty-five minor articles in the Encyclopaedia of Buddhism. He has published five books: A History of Indian Philosophy (Vol. 1); Causality: The Central Philosophy of Buddhism; Buddhist Philosophy: A Historical Analysis; The Way of Siddhartha (co-author Indrani Kalupahana); and Nagarjuna: The Philosophy of the Middle Way. He has taught at the University of Ceylon and at the University of Hawaii, where he is now Professor of Philosophy.

KAI NIELSEN (Ph.D., Duke University) is the author of many articles in the philosophy of religion, epistemology, and ethics. He has published Reason and Practice, Contemporary Critiques of Religion, Ethics Without God, Scepticism, An Introduction to the Philosophy of Religion, Equality and Liberty, In Defense of Atheism, and, most recently, Philosophy and Atheism. He has taught at Hamilton College, Amherst College, The State University of New York at Binghamton, Rhodes University, The University of Ottawa, The Graduate Center of the City University of New York, Brooklyn College, and New York University. A past president of the Canadian Philosophical Association, he is currently Professor of Philosophy and Head of the Department of Philosophy at the University of Calgary (Alberta, Canada).

NELSON PIKE (Ph.D., Harvard University) has published articles in the philosophy of religion, ethics, and the philosophy of mind, and is the author of God and Timelessness and the editor of both David Hume's Dialogues Concerning Natural Religion (which includes a lengthy commentary) and God and Evil: Readings on the Theological Problem of Evil. Pike has taught at the University of California, Los Angeles; Brown University; and Cornell University. He is currently Professor of Philosophy at the University of California, Irvine.

ALVIN PLANTINGA (Ph.D., Yale University) has published extensively in the philosophy of religion and metaphysics. He is the author of God and Other Minds; The Nature of Necessity; God, Freedom and Evil; and Does God Have a Nature?, and is the editor of Faith and Philosophy, The Ontological Argument, and (with Nicholas Wolterstorff) Faith and Rationality. Plantinga has been President of the American Philosophical Association, Western Division, and has taught at Wayne State University and Calvin College, in addition to being a Visiting Professor at a number of universities. He is currently J. O'Brien Professor of Philosophy at the University of Notre Dame (South Bend, Indiana).

JOSEPH RUNZO (Ph.D., University of Michigan; M.T.S., Harvard University) is the author of articles in the philosophy of religion, the philosophy of perception, and philosophical theology, which have appeared in such journals as The American Philosophical Quarterly, Religious Studies, The Scottish Journal of Theology, and The Heythrop Journal, and he is the author of Reason, Relativism, and God. Runzo is the founder and current President of the Philosophy of Religion Society and is Associate Professor of Philosophy and of Religion at Chapman College, California.

Introduction

The essays in this volume represent an important new direction in the philosophy of religion. Contemporary philosophers of religion have often concentrated on such issues as the validity and import of the classical arguments for God's existence, the meaning of the various divine attributes, the possibility of life after death, and the problem of evil. Recently, though, attention has begun to focus on fundamental questions in the epistemology of religion. The essays in this volume, written by some of the leading philosophers of religion, address basic questions about the general epistemic status of religious belief, questions which must first be answered if one eventually hopes to determine whether there is a firm, rational foundation for the specific claims and conceptions of actual religious belief and practice. Each of these papers was originally presented and discussed at a three-day conference on "Religion, Mysticism, and Knowledge" in the spring of 1981 at California State University, Fullerton. Most of the papers were subsequently revised for publication in the present volume.

The underlying issue which unifies these wide-ranging essays in the epistemology of religion is whether, and if so to what extent, an individual's religious experience could provide a proper basis or a justification for religious belief. Each author brings a distinctively different approach to this issue. Yet within this diversity of approach, the set of essays as a whole provides a mutually reinforcing and often directly interlocking analysis of this fundamental issue in the philosophy of religion. Of course, even with the advantage of diverse approaches, it is impossible to address every facet of the question of whether religious experience can provide a basis or justification for religious belief. But perhaps more important than their individual substantive answers to this foundational question, the authors of these essays help set the framework for new directions in this new focus on the epistemology of religion.

The essays of Plantinga, Nielsen, and Alston address the general issue of what sort of justification - if any - is requisite for religious belief. Can one rationally believe in God without having grounds which fully justify one's belief? Plantinga provides a carefully qualified positive answer to this question; Nielsen shows how certain sorts of "groundless" religious belief warrant skepticism about religion; and Alston specifically argues that religious experience can provide grounds to rationally justify religious belief.

xi

With these three general analyses of the nature of justification of religious belief setting the stage, as it were, the next two essays, those of Kalupahana and Pike, provide a more focused exploration of religious experience as a justifying basis for religious belief. Kalupahana presents a comparative study of the centrality of perceptual knowledge within the epistemology of two prominent figures in Eastern and Western religious thought: Buddha and William James. In his paper, Pike offers an even more focused analysis of the epistemic status of religious experience, by concentrating on the views of the great sixteenth-century Christian mystic, St. John of the Cross. Kalupahana's essay essentially provides a positive appraisal of religious experience as conveying knowledge; Pike's analysis of St. John of the Cross's position leads to a negative appraisal of the possible informational content of mystical experiences.

Finally, Hick and Runzo return to broader issues, and assess the implications for theological truth-claims of the thesis that religious experience provides the grounds for religious belief. Both authors argue from a basically Kantian epistemology that the content of all experience is conceptualized by, or structured by, the mind of the perceiver. Hick, confronting the fact of religious pluralism, suggests that the experiences of persons of different faiths lead to diverse and yet ultimately related insights into the nature of the divine. Runzo, confronting the emergence of relativism in modern theology, argues that an appeal to religious experience per se will fail to provide a non-relativistic, unencultured basis for religious belief.

Alvin Plantinga's essay, "On Taking Belief in God as Basic," is a bold defense against the view that it is irrational or unreasonable to hold theistic beliefs in the absence of sufficient supporting grounds or reasons. He argues against this "evidentialist objection" that (1) it is implausible to hold that there is an ultimate intellectual obligation not to believe in God without in fact having sufficient evidence, (2) we cannot have a prima facie intellectual duty not to believe in God without evidence since it is not usually within our power to simply cease believing things which we already believe, and (3) insofar as the evidentialist objection is based on classical foundationalism, it is based on a self-referentially incoherent view. Regarding (3), Plantinga suggests that the main tenet of classical foundationalism is that for any proposition, p, and any person, S,

(C) p is properly basic for S iff p is self-evident, incorrigible or evident to the senses for S.

But there do not seem to be good supporting arguments for (C), and if (C) itself is properly basic, then Plantinga points out according to (C), (C) must be either self-evident, incorrigible or evident to the senses, which it is not. Plantinga then argues that one can hold that belief in God is properly basic and yet not thereby commit oneself to a belief which is groundless or without

justifying circumstances. For just as perceptual experiences
provide the justification for beliefs such as "I see a tree," so
religious experiences provide the justification for belief in God.
And, Plantinga reasons, the criteria for the proper basicality of
beliefs is not any single necessary and sufficient condition (such
as (C)), but both varies with the kind of belief involved and must
be arrived at inductively. Thus, Christians will find the
criteria for the proper basicality of belief in God in examples of
experiences - the grounds for their belief - shared by the
Christian community.

Kai Nielsen takes an entirely different tack than Plantinga
in assessing the relevance of religious experience to religious
belief. He examines the prominent view held by those who follow
the later works of Wittgenstein that religion is a language-game
which, like all language-games, has internal criteria of
intelligibility and rational acceptability. On this view (held,
e.g., by D. Z. Phillips and Peter Winch), the fundamental beliefs
of the theist are not empirically testable or rationally
justifiable to those outside the language-game, via some set of
experiences. Against the Wittgensteinians, Nielsen insists that
the question "What does 'God' stand for?" is not a
pseudo-question, but a significant question which must be
answerable in terms of experience. Thus, Nielsen would agree with
Plantinga that religious belief does need some sort of justifying
experiential grounding. But Nielsen concludes that the questions
that "plain people ask" indicate that we do not know what we
believe in when we speak of believing in God. And skepticism
about religious belief, he contends, might be well-founded whether
or not religious belief needs justifying grounds.

In "Religious Experience as a Ground of Religious Belief,"
William Alston takes up the side of the justifiability of
religious belief. Arguing with precision and clarity, Alston
attempts to show that religious experience can provide direct
justification for religious belief. Through a comparison of sense
perception and religious experience, Alston defends "religious
empiricism" - the view that beliefs about acts of God directed
toward the recipient (comforting, strengthening, enlightening him
or her) are directly justified by religious experiences. Alston
distinguishes between a "normative" conception of justification
(having to do with our intellectual obligations) and a
"reliability" conception of justification (one having to do with
conduciveness to producing true beliefs). He then argues that
perceptual beliefs about our immediate environment are prima facie
justified if they arise from sense experiences which seem to the
perceiver to present the fact that is believed. But our perceptual
beliefs are only so justified in the weak normative sense that the
perceiver lacks adequate reasons for supposing that such beliefs,
when formed in this way, are unreliable. Alston then argues that
religious beliefs which are formed on the basis of religious
experience parallel perceptual beliefs formed on the basis of
sense experience in having the same, weaker sort of normative

justification. Commonly, religious experiences are discredited vis-a-vis perceptual experiences on the grounds that the former, unlike the latter, (1) offer no standard checks for accuracy, (2) offer no basis for the prediction of future events, (3) are not found universally among normal adults, and (4) are objectified by different perceivers using different conceptual schemes. Against this, Alston contends that there is no reason to suppose that features like (1)-(4) must be present to indicate the reliability of an epistemic practice. He ends his essay by pointing out that in fact we should expect (1)-(4) to be absent from religious experiences. For religious experiences, if veridical, are experiences of a being, God, Who is too "wholly other" for humans to grasp regularities in His behavior, or to achieve a comprehensive idea of His nature, and Who seems to allow His presence to be unmistakably clear only under very special circumstances.

Alston's analysis of the parallels between perceptual experience and religious experience provides a helpful bridge from the first three essays in the volume to the next two essays, which focus more closely on important classic views of the epistemic import of religious experience.

In the first essay, "The Epistemology of William James and Early Buddhism," David Kalupahana offers an unusual comparison of the Western thought of William James, a philosopher deeply concerned about the status of religious experience and belief, and the Eastern thought of the Buddha. Kalupahana begins by assessing James's overall epistemology, concentrating on his empiricism and, as part of his "radical empiricism," James's "anti-essentialism." This same strand of anti-essentialism which Kalupahana finds in James, the denial that we should "look for things as they are," he identifies in Buddha's doctrine of non-substantiality, the denial of a permanent and immutable substance in either the self or the world. Kalupahana then argues that the pragmatist approach of James, necessitated by his view of the impermanence of things, is also paralleled in the thought of Buddha. Thus, Kalupahana points to Buddha's view that while perceptual experience yields "mere knowledge" (not permanent knowledge which can be formulated into closed systems), yet it is only through immediate experience that we can understand things "as they are." This led Buddha to a non-absolutist view of truth which is not unlike James's relativistic, pragmatic conception of truth. And James's emphasis on immediate experience in religious matters, as well as in matters about the physical environment, accords with Buddha's emphasis on religious experience as opposed to dogma.

Nelson Pike gives this developing discussion of religious experience an even sharper focus in his provocative essay, "St. John of the Cross on Mystic Apprehensions as Sources of Knowledge." Pike analyzes St. John's contention that the individual experiences of mystics have no value as sources of information. He explicates St. John's position as the view not that the content of mystical experiences might be false, but that there is no way of determining precisely what the content is - i.e., that mystic apprehensions are opaque regarding their meaning.   Pike rejects St. John's own explanation of this phenomenon in terms of God's failure to communicate His intended message because He employs a kind of "code" not understood by the recipient.   Instead, Pike suggests that another explanation which St. John provides is more successful - viz., that mystic apprehensions are not "information-bearers" at all.   He ends his essay by considering the question, "If mystic apprehensions have no value as sources of propositional knowledge, what value do they have?" Comparing mystic visions to dreams, Pike suggests that the value of mystic apprehensions is an instructive awareness which is a causal result of the mystical experience.   The epistemic value of mystic experiences turns out to be, in Pike's words, a "cognitive wallop" rather than a set of propositions. If Pike is correct in his analysis of St. John's view, and if one accepts St. John's view of the epistemic status of mystical experiences, the question is left for the reader of how this will affect views like Plantinga's or Alston's that religious experiences can provide justifying grounds for religious beliefs.

With the two last essays by Hick and Runzo, we come full circle and again broaden the scope of the question whether, and if so to what extent, religious experience could provide a proper basis of justification for religious belief. Both authors discuss some of the wider implications of holding that religious belief can be properly grounded in religious experience.

John Hick addresses the knotty issue of religious pluralism in his essay "Towards a Philosophy of Religious Pluralism." What he calls the "basic religious conviction" that one's own religious experience and beliefs embody truths about the nature of the divine reality, together with the fact of religious pluralism, raises the problem of how one is to determine which of the various, apparently conflicting religious truth-claims are in fact correct. Hick proposes a scheme for understanding the relationship between individual religious experience, religious truth-claims, and the divine reality. Taking religious experience as of primary importance, Hick first distinguishes three basic types: (a) the experience of God as a personal presence, (b) what is usually referred to as the "nature" mystical experience, and (c) the experience in which the self is absorbed into the divine reality. Then, building from a Kantian model of experience in which all the "informational output" from external reality is interpreted via the mind's categorical system before "coming to consciousness as meaningful phenomenal experience," Hick develops the notion of an "image" of God.   Somewhat like the manner in which different historians have constructed different conceptions of a particular historical personage, people in different religious traditions have developed different "images" of God.   And just as our categorical systems determine, in part, the character of our sense experiences, so too religious experience is always experience in terms of a particular image of God. Thus, God is not known an

<u>sich</u>, but is known in relation to humankind and the images which we construct. Applying this analysis to the great world religions, Hick suggests that the plurality of the many traditions of religious experience provides a wider basis for theology than the limits of any one tradition of religious experience. Consequently, within the diverse "images" of God of the world religions, God can be understood, e.g., as personal or as non-personal, though all these images, Hick argues, are images of the one Godhead.

In the last essay, "Conceptual Relativism and Religious Experience," Runzo examines another feature of religious pluralism. He analyzes a general epistemological problem which will arise for any view which holds that religious experience provides the justification or justifying grounds for religious belief if, at the same time, conceptual relativism is taken seriously. For in response to religious pluralism, the acceptance of some form of relativism has been highly influential in twentieth-century theology. But this raises the question whether there is any way of avoiding enculturated, relative conceptions, in order to achieve an absolutist understanding of God which would satisfy religious faith. Runzo defines <u>conceptual</u> relativism as the epistemological position that "the <u>truth</u> of statements is relative to the conceptual schema(s) from within which they are formulated and/or assessed." He then suggests that within a conceptual relativist account, religious experience could not provide the basis for an absolutist understanding of the nature and acts of God. Runzo begins by arguing that the kind of attempts which Friedrich Schleiermacher and Martin Buber made to base true piety on direct religious experience will fail to evade this problem. He offers a "conceptualist" analysis of experience, reasoning that since all experience is radically conceptualized by the mind's ordering, the propositional content of religious experience will be inextricably delimited by the percipient's own conceptual schema. This will, given a conceptual relativist account of truth, inescapably relativize the propositional content of all religious experiences. Lastly, applying this analysis to mystical experiences in particular, Runzo argues that (1) whatever propositional content mystical experiences do have, that content will, if it is humanly understandable, be subject to the relativizing effect of the human recipient's conceptual schema, and (2) appeals to the ineffability of mystic experiences (thereby insulating them against conceptual relativism) are either incoherent or leave us, literally, with nothing to say.

It should be clear that the essays in this volume not only offer diverse and substantive analyses of whether, and to what extent, religious experience could provide a proper basis or justification for religious belief, but generate an internal debate on this issue: Plantinga and Alston suggest that religious experience could provide justifying grounds for religious belief; Nielsen raises a skeptical rejoinder. Kalupahana and Pike sharpen the focus on specific, classic views of the epistemic import of religious experience; Pike's analysis calls into question the notion that mystic apprehensions have value as bearers of propositional content. Hick and Runzo introduce the issue of the plurality of religious experience; but while Hick points to a unity of worldwide religious experience, Runzo raises the problem of relativism, an issue mentioned by Kalupahana and latent in Alston's observation that "it hardly requires mention that religious experience gets objectified in terms of radically different conceptual schemes in different religious traditions."

It should also be clear that the internal debate which these essays generate has a counterpart in the questions which these essays pose for continued work in the epistemology of religion. Plantinga leaves open the question of whether belief in God is in fact properly basic. Pike's essay raises the question (a question, for example, for Alston), whether ordinary religious experiences might fail, just like mystic experiences, to be information-bearers. Hick brings to the forefront the issue of what criteria might be used to determine which "image" of God is more adequate. Runzo's essay suggests that something in addition to religious experience is needed to make the substantive content of theology and faith (in some sense) absolute. This volume provides the framework for these new directions in the epistemology of religion.

Joseph Runzo   Chapman College, California

On Taking Belief in God as Basic
Alvin Plantinga

I. The Evidentialist Objection to Theistic Belief

Many philosophers - Clifford, Blanshard, Russell, Scriven, and Flew, to name a few - have argued that belief in God is irrational, or unreasonable, or not rationally acceptable, or intellectually irresponsible, or somehow noetically below par because, as they say, there is insufficient evidence for it (1). Bertrand Russell was once asked what he would say if, after dying, he were brought into the presence of God and asked why he hadn't been a believer. Russell's reply: "I'd say 'Not enough evidence God! Not enough evidence!'"(2). I don't know just how such a response would be received; but Russell, like many others, held that theistic belief is unreasonable because there is insufficient evidence for it. We all remember W. K. Clifford, that delicious enfant terrible, as William James called him, and his insistence that it is immoral, wicked, and monstrous, and maybe even impolite to accept a belief for which you don't have sufficient evidence:

> Who so would deserve well of his fellows in this matter will guard the purity of his belief with a very fanaticism of jealous care, lest at any time it should rest on an unworthy object, and catch a stain which can never be wiped away.

He adds that if a

> ...belief has been accepted on insufficient evidence, the pleasure is a stolen one. Not only does it deceive ourselves by giving us a sense of power which we do not really possess, but it is sinful, because it is stolen in defiance of our duty to mankind. That duty is to guard ourselves from such beliefs as from a pestilence which may shortly master our body and spread to the rest of the town.

and finally:

> To sum up: it is wrong always, everywhere, and for anyone to believe anything upon insufficient evidence.

1

(It is not hard to detect, in these quotations, the "tone of robustious pathos" with which James credits him.) Clifford, of course, held that one who accepts belief in God <u>does</u> accept that belief on insufficient evidence, and has indeed defied his duty to mankind. More recently, Bertrand Russell has endorsed the evidentialist injunction "Give to any hypothesis which is worth your while to consider, just that degree or credence which the evidence warrants."

More recently Anthony Flew (3) has commended what he calls Clifford's "luminous and compulsive essay" (perhaps 'compulsive' here is a misprint for 'compelling'); and Flew goes on to claim that there is, in his words a 'presumption of atheism.' What is a presumption of atheism, and why should we think there is one? Flew puts it as follows:

> The debate about the existence of God should properly begin from the presumption of atheism,...the onus of proof must lie upon the theist. The word 'atheism,' however, has in this contention to be construed unusually. Whereas nowadays the usual meaning of 'atheist' in English is 'someone who asserts there is no such being as God,' I want the word to be understood not positively but negatively. I want the original Greek preface 'a' to be read in the same way in 'atheist' as it is customarily read in such other Greco-English words as 'amoral,' 'atypical,' and 'asymmetrical.' In this interpretation an atheist becomes: not someone who positively asserts the non-existence of God; but someone who is simply not a theist.
>
> What the protagonist of my presumption of atheism wants to show is that the debate about the existence of God ought to be conducted in a particular way, and that the issue should be seen in a certain perspective. His thesis about the onus of proof involves that it is up to the theist: first to introduce and to defend his proposed concept of God; and second, to provide sufficient reason for believing that this concept of his does in fact have an application.

How shall we understand this? What does it mean, for example, to say that the debate "should properly begin from the presumption of atheism?" What sorts of things do debates begin from, and what is it for one to begin from such a thing? Perhaps Flew means something like this: to speak of where a debate should begin is to speak of the sorts of premises to which the affirmative and negative sides can properly appeal in arguing

2

their cases. Suppose you and I are debating the question whether, say, the United States has a right to seize Mideast oil fields if the OPEC countries refuse to sell us oil at what we think is a fair price. I take the affirmative, and produce for my conclusion an argument one premise of which is the proposition that the United States has indeed a right to seize these oil fields under those conditions. Doubtless that maneuver would earn me very few points. Similarly, a debate about the existence of God cannot sensibly start from the assumption that God does indeed exist. That is to say, the affirmative can't properly appeal, in its arguments, to such premises as that there is such a person as God; if she could, she'd have much too easy a time of it. So in this sense of 'start,' Flew is quite right: the debate can't start from the assumption that God exists.

Of course, it is also true that the debate can't start from the assumption that God does <u>not</u> exist; using 'atheism' in its ordinary sense, there is equally a presumption of aatheism (which, by a familiary principle of logic, reduces to theism). So it looks as if there is in Flew's sense a presumption of atheism, all right, but in that same sense an equal presumption of aatheism. If this is what Flew means, then what he says is entirely correct, if something of a truism.

In another passage, however, Flew seems to understand the presumption of atheism in quite another different fashion:

> It is by reference to this inescapable demand for grounds that the presumption of atheism is justified. If it is to be established that there is a God, then we have to have good grounds for believing that this is indeed so. Until or unless some such grounds are produced we have literally no reason at all for believing; and in that situation the only reasonable posture must be that of either the negative atheist or the agnostic.

Here we have the much more substantial suggestion that it is unreasonable or irrational to accept theistic belief in the absence of sufficient grounds or reasons. And of course Flew, along with Russell, Clifford and many others, holds that in fact there aren't sufficient grounds or evidence for belief in God. The evidentialist objection, therefore, appeals to the following two premises:

(A) It is irrational or unreasonable to accept theistic belief in the absence of sufficient evidence or reasons.

and

(B) There is no evidence or at any rate not sufficient evidence for the proposition that God exists.

3

(B), I think, is at best dubious. At present, however, I'm interested in the objector's other premise - the claim that it is irrational or unreasonable to accept theistic belief in the absence of evidence or reasons. Why suppose that's true? Why suppose a theist must have evidence or reason to think there is evidence for this belief, if he is not to be irrational? This isn't just obvious, after all.

Now many Reformed thinkers and theologians (4) have rejected natural theology (thought of as the attempt to provide proofs or arguments for the existence of of God). They have held not merely that the proffered arguments are unsuccessful, but that the whole enterprise is in some way radically misguided. In (B5), I argue that the Reformed rejection of natural theology is best construed as an inchoate and unfocused rejection of (A). What these Reformed thinkers really mean to hold, I think, is that belief in God is properly basic: it need not be based on argument or evidence from other propositions at all. They mean to hold that the believer is entirely within his intellectual right in believing as he does, even if he doesn't know of any good theistic argument (deductive or inductive), even if he doesn't believe that there is any such argument, and even if in fact no such argument exists. They hold that it is perfectly rational to accept belief in God without accepting it on the basis of any other beliefs or propositions at all. Why suppose that the believer must have evidence if he is not to be irrational? Why should anyone accept (A)? What is to be said in its favor?

Suppose we begin by asking what the objector means by describing a belief as irrational. What is the force of his claim that the theistic belief is irrational and how is it to be understood? The first thing to see is that this claim is rooted in a normative contention. It lays down conditions that must be met by anyone whose system of beliefs is rational; and here 'rational' is to be taken as a normative or evaluative term. According to the objector, there is a right way and a wrong way with respect to belief. People have responsibilities, duties and obligations with respect to their believings just as with respect to their actions - or if we think believings are a kind of action, their other actions. Professor Brand Blanshard puts this clearly:

> ...everywhere and always belief has an ethical aspect. There is such a thing as a general ethics of the intellect. The main principle of that ethic I hold to be the same inside and outside religion. This principle is simple and sweeping: Equate your assent to the evidence. (Reason and Belief, p. 401)

and according to Michael Scriven:

> Now even belief in something for which there

is no evidence, i.e., a belief which goes beyond the evidence, although a lesser sin that a belief in something which is contrary to well-established laws, is plainly irrational in that it simply amounts to attaching belief where it is not justified. So the proper alternative, when there is no evidence, is not mere suspension of belief, e.g., about Santa Claus, it is disbelief. It most certainly is not faith. (Primary Philosophy, p. 103).

Perhaps this sort of obligation is really a special case of a more general moral obligation; or perhaps, on the other hand, it is sui generis. In any event, says the objector, there are such obligations: to conform to them is to be rational and to go against them is to be irrational.

Now here the objector seems right; there are duties and obligations with respect to beliefs. One's own welfare and that of others sometimes depends on what one believes. If we're descending the Grand Teton and I'm setting the anchor for the 120-foot rappel into the Upper Saddle, I have an obligation to form such beliefs as this anchor point is solid only on the basis of careful scrutiny and testing. One comissioned to gather intelligence - the spies Joshua sent into Canaan, for example - has an obligation to get it right. I have an obligation with respect to the belief that Justin Martyr was a Latin apologist - an obligation arising from the fact that I teach Medieval philosophy, must make a declaration on this issue, and am obliged not to mislead my students here. The precise form of these obligations may be hard to specify: am I obliged to believe that J. M. was a Latin apologist if and only if J. M. was a Latin apologist? Or to form a belief on this topic only after the appropriate amount of checking and investigating? Or maybe just to tell the students the truth about it, whatever I myself believe in the privacy of my own study? Or to tell them what's generally thought by those who should know? In the rappel case: do I have a duty to believe that the anchor point is solid if and only if it is? Or just to check carefully before forming the belief? Or perhaps there's no obligation to believe at all, but only to act on a certain belief only after appropriate investigation. In any event, it seems plausible to hold that there are obligations and norms with respect to belief, and I do not intend to contest this assumption.

The objector begins, therefore, from the plausible contention that there are duties or obligations with respect to belief: call them "intellectual duties." These duties can be understood in several ways. First we could construe them teleologically; we could adopt an intellectual utilitarianism. Here the rough idea is that our intellectual obligations arise out of a connection between our beliefs and what is intrinsically good and intrinsically bad; and our intellectual obligations are just a special case of the general obligation so to act to maximize good and minimize evil. Perhaps this is how W. K Clifford thinks of the matter. If people accepted such propositions as this DC10 is airworthy when the evidence is insufficient, the consequences could be disastrous: so perhaps some of us, at any rate, have an obligation to believe that proposition only in the presence of adequte evidence. The intellectual utilitarian could be an ideal utilitarian; he could hold that certain epistemic states are intrinsically valuable - knowledge, perhaps, or believing the truth, or a skeptical and judicial temper that is not blown about by every wind of doctrine. Among our duties, then, is a duty to try to bring about these valuable states of affairs. Perhaps this is how Professor Chisholm is to be understood when he says

> Let us consider the concept of what might be called an "intellectual requirement." We may assume that every person is subject to a purely intellectual requirement: that of trying his best to bring it about that, for every proposition that he considers, he accepts it if and only if it is true. (Theory of Knowledge, 2nd ed., p. 9.)

Secondly, we could construe intellectual obligations aretetically; we could adopt what Professor Frankena calls a "mixed ethics of virtue" with respect to the intellect. There are valuable noetic or intellectual states (whether intrinsically or extrinsically valuable); there are also the corresponding intellectual virtues, the habits of acting so as to produce or promote or enhance those valuable states. One's intellectual obligations, then, are to try to produce and enhance these intellectual virtues in oneself and others.

Thirdly, we could construe intellectual obligations deontologically; we could adopt a pure ethics of obligation with respect to the intellect. Perhaps there are intellectual obligations that do not arise from any connection with good or evil, but attach to us just by virtue of our having the sorts of noetic powers human beings do in fact display. The above quotation from Chisholm could also be understood along these lines.

Intellectual obligations, therefore, can be understood teleologically or aretetically or deontologically. And perhaps there are purely intellectual obligations of the following sorts. Perhaps I have a duty not to take as basic a proposition whose denial seems self-evident. Perhaps I have a duty to take as basic the proposition I seem to see a tree under certain conditions. With respect to certain kinds of propositions, perhaps I have a duty to believe them only if I have evidence for them, and a duty to proportion the strength of my belief to the strength of my evidence.

6

Of course these would be prima facie obligations. One presumably has an obligation not to take bread from the grocery store without permission and another to tell the truth. Both can be overridden, in specific circumstances, by other obligations - in the first case, perhaps, an obligation to feed my starving children and in the second, an obligation to protect a human life. So we must distinguish prima facie duties or obligations from all-things-considered or on-balance (ultima facie?) obligations. I have a prima facie obligation to tell the truth; in a given situation, however, that obligation may be overridden by others, so that my duty, all things considered, is to tell a lie. This is the grain of truth contained in situation ethics and the ill-named "new morality."

And prima facie intellectual obligations can conflict, just as obligations of other sorts. Perhaps I have a prima facie obligation to believe what seems to me self-evident, and what seems to me to follow self-evidently from what seems to me self-evident. But what if, as in the Russell paradoxes, something that seems self-evidently false apparently follows, self-evidently, from what seems self-evidently true? Here prima facie intellectual obligations conflict, and no matter what I do, I will violate a prima facie obligation. Another example: in reporting the Grand Teton rappel, I neglected to mention the violent electrical storm coming in from the southwest; to escape it we must get off in a hurry, so that I have a prima facie obligation to inspect the anchor point carefully, but anchor to set up the rappel rapidly, which means I can't spend a lot of time inspecting the anchor point.

Thus lightly armed, suppose we return to the evidential objector. Does he mean to hold that the theist without evidence is violating some intellectual obligation? If so, which one? Does he claim, for example, that the theist is violating his ultima facie intellectual obligation in thus believing? Perhaps he thinks anyone who believes in God without evidence is violating his all-things-considered intellectual duty. This, however, seems unduly harsh. What about the 14-year-old theist brought up to believe in God in a community where everyone believes? This 14-year-old theist, we may suppose, doesn't believe on the basis of evidence. He doesn't argue thus: everyone around here says God loves us and cares for us; most of what everyone around here says is true; so probably that's true. Instead, he simply believes what he's taught. Is he violating an all-things-considered intellectual duty? Surely not. And what about the mature theist - Thomas Aquinas, let's say - who thinks he does have adequate evidence? Let's suppose he's wrong; let's suppose all of his arguments are failures. Nevertheless, he has reflected long, hard and conscientiously on the matter and thinks he does have adequate evidence. Shall we suppose he's violating an all-things-considered intellectual duty here? I should think not. So construed, the objector's contention is totally implausible.

Perhaps, then, he is to be understood as claiming that there

7

is a prima facie intellectual duty not to believe in God without evidence. This duty can be overridden by circumstances, of course; but there is a prima facie obligation to believe propositions of this sort only on the basis of evidence. But here too there are problems. The suggestion is that I now have the prima facie obligation to believe propositions of this sort only on the basis of evidence. I have a prima facie duty to comply with the following command: either have evidence or don't believe. But this may be a command I can't comply with. The objector thinks there isn't adequate evidence for this belief, so presumably I can't have adequate evidence for it, unless we suppose I could create some. And it is also not within my power to refrain from believing this proposition. My beliefs aren't for the most part directly within my control. If you order me now, for example, to cease believing that the earth is very old, there's no way I can comply with your order. But in the same way it isn't within my power to cease believing in God now. So this alleged prima facie duty is one such that it isn't within my power to comply with it. But how can I have a prima facie duty to do what it isn't within my power to do?

Presumably, then, the objector means to be understood in still another fashion. Although it is not within my power now to cease believing now, there may be a series of actions now, such that I can now take the first, and after taking the first, will be able to take the second, and so on; and after taking the whole series of actions, I will no longer believe in God. Perhaps the objector thinks it is my prima facie duty to undertake whatever sort of regimen will at some time in the future result in my not believing without evidence. Perhaps I should attend a Universalist Unitarian Church, for example, and consort with members of the Rationalist Society of America. Perhaps I should read a lot of Voltaire and Bertrand Russell. Even if I can't now stop believing without evidence, perhaps there are other actions I can now take, such that if I do take them, then at some time in the future I won't be in this deplorable condition.

There is still another option available to the objector. He need not hold that the theist without evidence is violating some duty, prima facie, ultima facie or otherwise. Consider someone who believes that Venus is smaller than Mercury, not because he has evidence, but because he finds it amusing to believe what everyone disbelieves - or consider someone who holds this belief on the basis of an outrageously bad argument. Perhaps there is no obligation he has failed to meet; nevertheless his intellectual condition is defective in some way; or perhaps alternatively there is a commonly achieved excellence he fails to display. Perhaps he is like someone who is easily gulled, or walks with a limp, or has a serious astigmatism, or is unduly clumsy. And perhaps the evidentialist objection is to be understood, not as the claim that the theist without evidence has failed to meet some obligation, but that he suffers from a certain sort of intellectual deficiency. If this is the objector's view, then his proper

8

attitude towards the theist would be one of sympathy rather than censure.

These are some of the ways, then, in which the evidentialist objection could be developed; and of course there are still other possibilities. For ease of exposition, let us take the claim deontologically; what I shall say will apply mutatis mutandis if we take it one of the other ways. The viedentialist objector, then, holds that it is irrational to believe in God without evidence. He doesn't typically hold, however, that the same goes for every proposition; for given certain plausible conditions on the evidence relation it would follow that if we believe anything, then we are under obligation to believe infinitely many propositions. Let's say that proposition p is basic for a person S if S believes p but does not have evidence for p; and let's say that p is properly basic for S if S is within his epistemic rights in taking p as basic. The viedentialist objection, therefore, presupposes some view as to what sorts of propositions are correctly or rightly or justifiably taken as basic; it presupposes a view as to what is properly basic. And the minimally relevant claim for the evidentialist objector is that belief in God is not properly basic. Typically this objection has been rooted in some form of classical foundationalism, an enormously popular picture or total way of looking at faith, knowledge, justified belief, rationality and allied topics. This picture had been widely accepted ever since the days of Plato and Aristotle; its near relatives, perhaps, remain the dominant ways of thinking about these topics. According to the classical foundationalist, some propositions are properly or rightly basic for a person and some are not. Those that are not, are rationally accepted only on the basis of evidence where the evidence must trace back, ultimately, to what is properly basic. Now there are two varieties of classical foundationalism. According to the ancient and medieval variety, a proposition is properly basic for a person S if and only if it is either self-evident to S or 'evident to the senses,' to use Aquinas's term for S; according to the modern variety, a proposition is properly basic for S if and only if it is either self-evident to S or incorrigible for him. For ease of exposition, let's say that classical foundationalism is the disjunction of ancient and medieval with modern foundationalism; according to the classical foundationalist, then, a proposition is properly basic for a person S if and only if it is either self-evident to S or incorrigible for S or evident to the senses for S.

Now I said that the evidentialist objection to theistic belief is typically rooted in classical foundationalism. Insofar as it is so rooted, it is poorly rooted. For classical foundationalism is self-referentially incoherent. Consider the main tenet of classical foundationalism:

(C) p is properly basic for S if and only if p
     is self-evident, incorrigible or evident to

9

the senses for S.

Now of course the classical foundationalist accepts (C) and proposes that we do so as well. And either he takes (C) as basic or he doesn't. If he doesn't, then if he is rational in accepting it, he must by his own claims have an argument for it from propositions that are properly basic, by argument forms whose corresponding conditionals are properly basic. Classical foundationalists do not, so far as I know, offer such arguments for (C). I suspect the reason is that they don't know of any arguments of that sort for (C). It is certainly hard to see what such an argument would be. Accordingly, classical foundationalists probably take (C) as basic. But then according to (C) itself, if (C) is properly taken as basic, it must be either self-evident, incorrigible or evident to the senses for the foundationalist, and clearly it isn't any of those. If the foundationalist takes (C) as basic, therefore, he is self-referentially inconsistent. We must conclude, I think, that the classical foundationalist is in self-referential hot water - his own acceptance of the central tenet of his view is irrational by his own standards.

II. Objections to Taking Belief in God As Basic

Insofar as the evidentialist objection is rooted in classical foundationalism, it is poorly rooted indeed; and so far as I know, no one has developed and articulated any other reason for supporting that belief in God is not properly basic. Of course it doesn't follow that it is properly basic; perhaps the class of properly basic propositions is broader than classical foundationalists think, but still not broad enough to admit belief in God. But why think so? What might be the objections to the Reformed view that belief in God is properly basic?

I've heard it argued that if I have no evidence for the existence of God, then if I accept that proposition, my belief will be groundless, or gratuitous, or arbitrary. I think this is an error; let me explain.

Suppose we consider perceptual beliefs, memory beliefs, and beliefs ascribing mental states to other persons: such beliefs as

(1) I see a tree;

(2) I had breakfast this morning; and

(3) That person is angry.

Although beliefs of this sort are typically and properly taken as basic, it would be a mistake to describe them as groundless. Upon having experience of a certain sort, I believe that I am perceiving a tree. In the typical case I do not hold this belief

10

on the basis of other beliefs; it is nonetheless not groundless. My having that characteristic sort of experience - to use Professor Chisholm's language, my being appeared treely to - plays a crucial role in the formation and justification of that belief. We might say this experience, together, perhaps, with other circumstances, is what <u>justifies</u> me in holding it; this is the <u>ground</u> of my justification, and, by extension, the ground of the belief itself.

If I see someone displaying typical pain behavior, I take it that he or she is in pain. Again, I don't take the displayed behavior as <u>evidence</u> for that belief; I don't infer that belief from others <u>I hold</u>; I don't accept it on the basis of other beliefs. Still, my perceiving the pain behavior plays a unique role in the formation and justification of that belief; as in the previous case, it forms the ground of my justification for the belief in question. The same holds for memory beliefs. I seem to remember having breakfast this morning; that is, I have an inclination to believe the proposition that I had breakfast, along with a certain past-tinged experience that is familiar to all but hard to describe. Perhaps we should say that I am appeared to pastly; but perhaps that insufficiently distinguishes the experience in question from that accompanying beliefs about the past not grounded in my own memory. The phenomenology of memory is a rich and unexplored realm; here I have no time to explore it. In this case as in the others, however, there is a justifying circumstance present, a condition that forms the ground of my justification for accepting the memory belief in question.

In each of these cases, a belief is taken as basic, and in each case properly taken as basic. In each case there is some circumstance or condition that confers justification; there is a circumstance that serves as the <u>ground</u> of justification. So in each case there will be some true proposition of the sort:

(4) In condition <u>C</u>, <u>S</u> is justified in taking <u>p</u> as basic. Of course <u>C</u> will vary with <u>p</u>.

For a perceptual judgment such as

(5) I see a rose-colored wall before me,

<u>C</u> will include my being appeared to in a certain fashion. No doubt <u>C</u> will include more. If I'm appeared to in the familiar fashion but know that I am wearing rose-colored glasses, or that I am suffering from a disease that causes me to be thus appeared to, no matter what the color of the nearby objects, then I am not justified in taking (5) as basic. Similarly for memory. Suppose I know that my memory is unreliable; it often plays me tricks. In particular, when I seem to remember having breakfast, then, more often than not, I <u>haven't</u> had breakfast. Under these conditions I am not justified <u>in taking</u> it as basic that I had breakfast, even though I seem to remember that I did.

11

So being appropriately appeared to, in the perceptual case, is not sufficient for justification; some further condition - a condition hard to state in detail - is clearly necessary. The central point, here, however, is that a belief is properly basic only in certain conditions; these conditions are, we might say, the ground of its justification and, by extension, the ground of the belief itself. In this sense, basic beliefs are not, or are not necessarily, groundless beliefs.

Now similar things may be said about belief in God. When the Reformers claim that this belief is properly basic, they do not mean to say, of course, that there are no justifying circumstances for it, or that it is in that sense groundless or gratuitous. Quite the contrary. Calvin holds that God "reveals and daily discloses himself in the whole workmanship of the universe," and the divine art "reveals itself in the innumerable and yet distinct and well-ordered variety of the heavenly host." God has so created us that we have a tendency or disposition to see his hand in the world about us. More precisely, there is in us a disposition to believe propositions of the sort this flower was created by God or this vast and intricate universe was created by God when we contemplate the flower or behold the starry heavens or think about the vast reaches of the universe.

Calvin recognizes, at least implicitly, that other sorts of conditions may trigger this disposition. Upon reading the Bible, one may be impressed with a deep sense that God is speaking to him. Upon having done what I know is cheap, or wrong, or wicked, I may feel guilty in God's sight and form the belief God disapproves of what I've done. Upon confession and repentance, I may feel forgiven, forming the belief God forgives me for what I've done. A person in grave danger may turn to God, asking for His protection and help; and of course he or she then forms the belief that God is indeed able to hear and help if He sees fit. When life is sweet and satisfying, a spontaneous sense of gratitude may well up within the soul; someone in this condition may thank and praise the Lord for His goodness, and will of course form the accompanying belief that indeed the Lord is to be thanked and praised.

There are therefore many conditions and circumstances that call forth belief in God: guilt, gratitude, danger, a sense of God's presence, a sense that He speaks, perception of various parts of the universe. A complete job would explore the phenomenology of all these conditions and of more besides. This is a large and important topic; but here I can only point to the existence of these conditions.

Of course none of the beliefs I mentioned a moment ago is the simple belief that God exists. What we have instead are such beliefs as

(6) God is speaking to me;

(7) God has created all this;

(8) God disapproves of what I have done;

(9) God forgives me; and

(10) God is to be thanked and praised.

These propositions are properly basic in the right circumstances. But it is quite consistent with this to suppose that the proposition <u>there is such a person as God</u> is neither properly basic nor taken as basic by those who believe in God. Perhaps what they take as basic are such propositions as (6)-(10), believing in the existence of God on the basis of such propositions. From this point of view, it isn't exactly right to say that it is belief in God that is properly basic; more exactly, what are properly basic are such propositions (6)-(10), each of which self-evidently entails that God exists. It isn't the relatively high level and general proposition <u>God exists</u> that is properly basic, but instead propositions detailing some of His attributes or actions.

Suppose we return to the analogy between belief in God and belief in the existence of perceptual objects, other persons, and the past. Here too it is relatively specific and concrete propositions rather than their more general and abstract colleagues that are properly basic. Perhaps such items as

(11) There are trees;

(12) There are other persons; and

(13) The world has existed for more than 5 minutes

are not properly basic; it is instead such propositions as

(14) I see a tree;

(15) That person is pleased; and

(16) I had breakfast more than an hour ago

that deserve accolade. Of course propositions of the latter sort immediately and self-evidently entail propositions of the former sort; and perhaps there is thus no harm in speaking of the former as properly basic, even though so to speak is to speak a bit loosely.

The same must be said about belief in God. We may say, speaking loosely, that belief in God is properly basic; strictly speaking, however, it is probably not that proposition but such propositions as (6)-(10) that enjoy that status. But the main point, here, is this: belief in God or (6)-(10) are properly basic; to say so, however, is not to deny that there are justifying conditions for these beliefs, or conditions that confer justification on one who accepts them as basic. They are therefore not groundless or gratuitous.

A second objection I've often heard: if belief in God is properly basic, why can't just any belief be properly basic? What about voodoo or astrology? What about the belief that the Great Pumpkin returns every Halloween? Could I properly take that as basic? And if I can't, why can I properly take belief in God as basic? Suppose I believe that if I flap my arms with sufficient vigor, I can take off and fly about the room; could I defend myself against the charge of irrationality by claiming this belief is basic? If we say that belief in God is properly basic, won't we be committed to holding that just anything, or nearly anything, can properly be taken as basic, thus throwing wide the gates to irrationalism and superstition?

Certainly not. What might lead one to think the Reformed epistemologist is in this kind of trouble? The fact that he rejects the criteria for proper basicality purveyed by classical foundationalism? But why should that be thought to commit him to such tolerance or irrationality? Consider an analogy. In the palmy days of positivism, the positivists went about confidently wielding their verifiability criterion and declaring meaningless much that was obviously meaningful. Now suppose someone rejected a formulation of that criterion - the one to be found in the second edition of A. J. Ayer's Language, Truth and Logic, for example. Would that mean she was committed to holding that

(17) T'was brilling; and the slithy toves did gyre
     and gymble in the wabe

contrary to appearances, makes good sense? Of course not. But then the same goes for the Reformed epistemologist; the fact that he rejects the Classical Foundationalist's criterion of proper basicality does not mean that he is committed to supposing just anything is properly basic.

But what then is the problem? Is it that the Reformed epistemologist not only rejects those criteria for proper basicality, but seems in no hurry to produce what he takes to be a better substitute? If he has no such criterion, how can he fairly reject belief in the Great Pumpkin as properly basic?

This objection betrays an important misconception. How do we rightly arrive at or develop criteria for meaningfulness, or justified belief, or proper basicality? Where do they come from? Must one have such a criterion before one can sensibly make any judgments - positive or negative - about proper basicality? Surely not. Suppose I don't know of a satisfactory substitute for the criteria proposed by Classical Foundationalism; I am nevertheless entirely within my rights in holding that certain propositions are not properly basic in certain conditions. Some propositions seem self-evident when in fact they are not; that is the lesson of some of the Russell paradoxes. Nevertheless it would be irrational to take as basic the denial of a proposition that seems self-evident to you. Similarly, suppose it seems to you that you see a tree; you would then be irrational in taking as basic the proposition that you don't see a tree, or that there aren't any trees. In the same way, even if I don't know of some illuminating criterion of meaning, I can quite properly declare (17) meaningless.

And this raises an important question - one Roderick Chisholm has taught us to ask. What is the status of the criteria for knowledge, or proper basicality, or justified belief? Typically, these are universal statements. The modern foundationalist's criterion for proper basicality, for example, is doubly universal:

> (18) For any proposition A and person S, A is
> properly basic for S if and only if A is
> incorrigible for S or self-evident to S.

But how could one know a thing like that? What are its credentials? Clearly enough, (18) isn't self-evident or just obviously true. But if it isn't, how does one arrive at it? What sorts of arguments would be appropriate? Of course a foundationalist might find (18) so appealing, he simply takes it to be true, neither offering argument for it, nor accepting it on the basis of other things he believes. If he does so, however, his noetic structure will be self-referentially incoherent. (18) itself is neither self-evident nor incorrigible; hence in accepting (18) as basic, the modern foundationalist violates the condition of proper basicality he himself lays down in accepting it. On the other hand, perhaps the foundationalist will try to produce some argument for it from premises that are self-evident or incorrigible: it is exceedingly hard to see, however, what such an argument might be like. And until he has produced such arguments, what shall the rest of us do - we who do not find (18) at all obvious or compelling? How could he use (18) to show us that belief in God, for example, is not properly basic? Why should we believe (18), or pay it any attention?

The fact is, I think, that neither (18) nor any other revealing necessary and sufficient condition for proper basicality follows from clearly self-evident premises by clearly acceptable arguments. And hence the proper way to arrive at such a criterion is, broadly speaking, _inductive_. We must assemble examples of beliefs and conditions such that the former are obviously properly basic in the latter, and examples of beliefs and conditions such that the former are obviously _not_ properly basic in the latter. We must then frame hypotheses as to the necessary and sufficient conditions of proper basicality and test these hypotheses by reference to those examples. Under the right conditions, for example, it is clearly rational to believe that you see a human person before you: a being who has thoughts and feelings, who knows and believes things, who makes decisions and acts. It is clear, furthermore, that you are under no obligation to reason to

15

this belief from others you hold; under those conditions that belief is properly basic for you. But then (18) must be mistaken; the belief in question, under those circumstances, is properly basic, though neither self-evident nor incorrigible for you. Similarly, you may seem to remember that you had breakfast this morning, and perhaps you know of no reason to suppose your memory is playing you tricks. If so, you are entirely justified in taking that belief as basic. Of course it isn't properly basic on the criteria offered by classical foundationalists; but that fact counts not against you but against those criteria.

Accordingly, criteria for proper basicality must be reached from below rather than above; they should not be presented as obiter dicta, but argued to and tested by a relevant set of examples. But there is no reason to assume, in advance, that everyone will agree on the examples. The Christian will of course suppose that belief in God is entirely proper and rational; if he doesn't accept this belief on the basis of other propositions, he will conclude that it is basic for him and quite properly so. Followers of Bertrand Russell and Madelyn Murray O'Hare may disagree, but how is that relevant? Must my criteria, or those of the Christian community, conform to their examples? Surely not. The Christian community is responsible to its set of examples, not to theirs.

Accordingly, the Reformed epistemologist can properly hold that belief in the Great Pumpkin is not properly basic, even though he holds that belief in God is properly basic and even if he has no full-fledged criterion of proper basicality. Of course he is committed to supposing that there is a relevant difference between belief in God and belief in the Great Pumpkin, if he holds that the former, but not the latter, is properly basic. But this should prove no great embarrassment; there are plenty of candidates. These candidates are to be found in the neighborhood of the conditions I mentioned in the last section that justify and ground belief in God. Thus, for example, the Reformed epistemologist may concur with Calvin in holding that God has implanted in us a natural tendency to see his hand in the world around us; the same cannot be said for the Great Pumpkin, there being no Great Pumpkin and no natural tendency to accept beliefs about the Great Pumpkin.

By way of conclusion then: being self-evident, or incorrigible, or evident to the senses is not a necessary condition of proper basicality. Furthermore, one who holds that belief in God is properly basic is not thereby committed to the idea that belief in God is groundless or gratuitous or without justifying circumstances. And even if he lacks a general criterion of proper basicality, he is not obliged to suppose that just any, or nearly any, belief - belief in the Great Pumpkin, for example - is properly basic. Like everyone should, he begins with examples; and he may take belief in the Great Pumpkin, in certain circumstances, as a paradigm of irrational basic belief.

16

NOTES

1. See for example (B1), pp. 400f; (B2), pp. 345f; (B3), p. 22; (B6), pp. 3ff; and (B7), pp. 87ff. In (B4) I consider and reject the evidentialist objection to theistic belief.

2. W. Salmon, "Religion and Science: A New Look at Hume's Dialogues," Philosophical Studies 33 (1978), p. 176.

3. A. G. N. Flew, The Presumption of Atheism (London: Pemberton Publishing Co., 1976).

4. A Reformed thinker or theologian is one whose intellectual sympathies lie with the Protestant tradition going back to John Calvin (not someone who was formerly a theologian and has since seen the light).

BIBLIOGRAPHY

(B1) Blanshard, Brand. Reason and Belief (London: Allen & Urwin, 1974).

(B2) Clifford, W. K. "The Ethics of Belief," in Lectures and Essays (London: MacMillan, 1879).

(B3) Flew, A. G. N. The Presumption of Atheism (London: Pemberton Publishing Co., 1976).

(B4) Plantinga, A. "Is Belief in God Rational?" in Rationality and Religious Belief, ed. C. Delaney (Indiana: University of Notre Dame Press, 1979).

(B5) Plantinga, A. "The Reformed Objection to Natural Theology," in Proceedings of the American Catholic Philosophical Association (1980).

(B6) Russell, Bertrand. "Why I Am Not a Christian,' in Why I Am Not a Christian (New York: Simon & Schuster, 1957).

(B7) Scriven, Michael. Primary Philosophy, (New York: McGraw-Hill, 1966).

Published in Faith and Rationality, eds. Alvin Plantinga and Nicholas Wolterstorff (South Bend, Indiana: University of Notre Dame Press, 1984). This condensed and adapted version reprinted by permission of University of Notre Dame Press.)

Religion and Groundless Believing
Kai Nielsen

It is a fundamental religious belief of Jews and Christians that a human being's chief end is to glorify God and to enjoy Him forever. Human beings are not simply creatures who will rot and die but they will survive the death of their present bodies. They will, after the Last Judgment, if they are saved, come into a blissful union with God, free finally of all sin, and they will be united in Heaven in human brotherhood and love. But for now, that is in our 'earthly' condition of life. We stand in division both inwardly as self-divided creatures and against each other as well; a kingdom of heaven on earth is far from being realized. We humans - or so Jews and Christians believe - are sinful creatures standing before the God of mercy and love, of whose forgiveness we stand in need and to whom everything is owed.

The thing we see here is that being a Jew or Christian is not just the having of one framework-belief, namely a belief that there is a God. And it is not just, as some philosophers seem to assume, the having of that belief and the having of another, namely that we will survive the death of our bodies. Rather, as Wittgenstein and Malcolm stress, what we have with a religion is a system, or as I would prefer to call it, a cluster of interlocking beliefs, qualifying and giving each other sense and mutual support (1). We have here a world-picture which not only tells us, or purports to tell us, what is the case but orients and guides our lives and can touch profoundly - if we can accept such a world-picture - our hopes and expectations as well. To be a Jew or a Christian is to be a person whose sense of self and sense of the meaningfulness of life are tied up with that world-picture.

It has seemed to many philosophers, believers and non-believers alike, that key concepts in this world-picture - God, heaven, hell, sin, the Last Judgment, a human being's chief end, being resurrected and coming to be a new man with a new body - are all in one degree or another problematic conceptions whose very intelligibility or rational acceptability are not beyond reasonable doubt. Yet it is just this skeptical thrust - or so at least it would appear - that Wittgenstein and certain Wittgensteinians oppose as itself a product of <u>philosophical</u> confusion (2). In the systemic home of various ongoing and deeply entrenched language-games, these concepts have a place and in that context they are, and must be, perfectly in order as they are. Within those language-games no genuine questions of their intelligibility or rational acceptability can arise, and criticisms from the outside - from the vantage point of some other language-game - are always irrelevant, for the criteria of intelligibility or rational acceptability are always in part dependent on a particular language-game (3). It might be thought that the phrase 'genuine question' in the above is a tip-off marking what in effect is a persuasive definition and showing, as clearly as can be, that questions can and do arise over such general criteria within the parameters of such language-games. But the response would be that no one who commanded a clear view of what she or he was saying and doing would try to make such a challenge or search for such general criteria of intelligibility or rationality, for she would be perfectly aware that she had no place to stand in trying to gain such a critical vantage point. There just are no criteria of intelligibility or rationality uberhaupt (4). Such a person has, and can have, no Archimedean point in accordance with which she could carry out such a critique.

Genuine criticism, such Wittgensteinians argue, will have to proceed piecemeal and within the parameters of these different but often interlocking language-games. Critique, if it is to cut deeply and be to the point, must be concrete (specific) and involve an extended examination of the forms of life from within. For such a criticism to be a genuine possibility, the critics must have a sensitive participant's (or participant-like) understanding of these forms of life as they are exhibited in the language-games with which they are matched. (Perhaps it is more adequate to say the language-games are embedded in forms of life!)

In such a context criticism is in order and is an indispensable tool in the development of a tradition, but there is - so the claim goes - no genuinely relevant criticism possible of language-games as a whole or of forms of life. There is no coherent sense, such Wittgensteinians argue, in which we can speak of a confused language-game or an irrational form of life, or of a full-fledged conceptually distinct practice which is irrational or incoherent (5). Our language-games are rooted in these practices and are not in need of justification or of a foundation. In fact the whole idea of foundations or grounds or justification here is without sense. Foundationalism is a philosophical mythology. There is no logic which can give us the a priori order of the world. Rather, our logical distinctions are found in, or become a codification of, distinctions found in our various language-games. But the sense - the intelligibility - of our language-games cannot be coherently questioned. There is, they claim, no coherent sense to the phrase 'a confused language-game' or 'a confused but conceptually distinct practice' or 'an irrational form of life.' We indeed have a deep philosophical penchant to go on to question, to ask for foundations for, to try to justify, such practices, language-games or forms of life. But it is just here where we fall into transcendental illusion. We do not recognize the import of Wittgenstein's full stop and we dream of justification where none exists or even could exist.

Both understanding and genuine criticism must, initially at least, proceed by seeing how the various concepts interlock and

how in the form of a whole system - a cluster of concepts - they
make sense. There is no understanding them in isolation. We come
to understand their use by coming to see their place - their
various roles - in the system. There is no understanding 'the
chief end of man' outside of something like a religious context,
and there is no understanding the distinctive end of man
envisioned by Christianity without understanding its concept of
God. And there is, so the claim goes, no even tolerable
understanding of Christianity's concept of God without
understanding the Christian concept of the end of man and man's
highest good. And in turn to understand that, it is necessary to
make sense of a man's surviving the death of his present body and
coming to have a resurrection body in a resurrection world. There
is no more breaking away the Christian conception of the end of
man or man's highest good from such cosmological conceptions than
there is a way of breaking away the conception of the Last
Judgment from them. And in turn the concepts of heaven, blissful
union with God, human brotherhood, love and sin do not stand on
their own feet but gain their distinctively Christian sense from
their interlocking with these other concepts of Christian life.
These concepts and many others like them cluster together, and we
cannot understand them in isolation. Moreover, they stand and
fall together.

II

Yet, these critical Wittgensteinian points notwithstanding,
there is a certain probing of those concepts which is quite
natural and which can - or so it at least appears - be carried out
in relative isolation from the examination of the other concepts
of the cluster, provided we have something like a participant's
grasp of the whole cluster. In wondering about the resurrection
body in the resurrection world, we naturally wonder how identity
is preserved in the resurrection or reconstitution of the body.
Who is it that is me in the interim between the decay of the 'old
body' and the emergence of 'the new one,' and in what space and in
what world in relation to our present familiar world of everyday
life and physics is this resurrection world? Is it even logically
or conceptually possible for a rocket to be shot up to it?
Somehow this all seems fatuous - a plain getting of it wrong - but
what then is a getting of it right, what is it that we are talking
about, and does it make sense? Does it help our understanding at
all to say that we must just understand it in its own terms? Does
it help particularly the perplexities we feel at this juncture to
relate such conceptions to the other conceptions in our religious
language-game? It is not at all clear to me that, about these
particular worries, it does help much, if at all, to relate these
philosophically perplexing conceptions to other religious
conceptions.

21

Even more important is the role of the concept of God here. While gaining its meaning in a certain determinate context in a cluster of concepts, the concept of God can still have, in relative isolation, certain questions addressed to it. We glorify God and find our chief joy in Him, but who or what is this God we enjoy, and how appropriate is the use of personal pronouns in such talk? We have the word 'God,' but is it a proper name, an abbreviated definite description, a special kind of descriptive predicate or what? It surely appears to be some kind of referring expression, but what does it refer to? How could we be acquainted with, or could we be acquainted with or otherwise come to know, what it stands for or characterizes? How do we - or do we - identify God, how do we individuate God, what are we talking about when we talk of God, do we succeed in making any successful reference when we speak of God? What or who is this God we pray to, love, find our security in, make sense of our lives in terms of, and the like? Our cluster of religious concepts will help us somewhat here. We know He is the God of love, who transcends in His might and mystery our paltry understandings. Some Jews and Christians believe He is that being whom we will somehow meet face-to-face when we are resurrected and our sins are washed away; and we know that He is a being of infinite mercy and love, with whom we may somehow, someday be in blissful union in a world without division, strife, or alienation, where love and brotherhood (sisterhood) prevail.

This helps to some extent to locate God in conceptual space, but only to some extent, for still the nagging question persists: what is it or who is it that is this being of infinite love, mercy, power and understanding, of whom we stand in need? What literally are we talking about when we speak of this being? Of what kind of reality or putative reality do we speak when we speak of, or even talk to, God? (If we have no conception of what it is to speak literally here, then we can have no understanding of the possibility of speaking metaphorically or analogically either, for the possibility of the latter is parasitic on the possibility of the former.) Suppose someone says there is no reality here, that 'God' answers to nothing at all - stands for, makes reference to, nothing at all. How are we to answer him and show he is mistaken? And how are we to answer the other chap who looks on the scene and says he does not know how to decide such an issue? He does not understand what it would be like to succeed in making reference to 'God,' but not knowing that, he also does not know - indeed cannot know - that 'God' does not stand for anything either. If we don't understand what could count as success, how could we understand what could count as failure? All these people can play Jewish or Christian language-games with such a cluster of concepts, but they remain thoroughly perplexed about what, if anything, they are talking about in speaking of God. If that is so, how can we possibly be justified in saying that the concepts in question are unproblematic and are in order as they are? We know what it is that religious people do with such words; we can do similar things

with words as well, and we understand full well the uses of
language involved. We could do it all quite competently in a play
if necessary. But though we can speak and act and at least seem
to share a common understanding, we cannot decide on whether 'God'
does, or even could (given its meaning) secure reference - stand
for something, refer to something actually real - and we do not
agree about or understand how to go about settling or resolving or
even dissolving that issue. But how then can these key concepts
or conceptions be unproblematic?

III

Some, whom I have perhaps tendentiously called
Wittgensteinian Fideists, would respond that the core mistake in
what I have been arguing about is that I continue to construe God
as an object or a thing or entity of some sort. That this is a
governing assumption for me, as it is for Flew as well, is
revealed in our repeated request for a specification of the
referent (denotation) of 'God,' in our asking repeatedly who or
what is God (6). We both are, it could be argued, looking for the
substance answering to the substantive, and sometimes at least
that is a mistake of such an order as to show a fundamental
confusion about the logic of God. It confuses the surface grammar
of the concept with its depth grammar.
There is no more question, they claim, of finding out whether
God exists than there is of finding out whether physical objects
exist. The putative question 'Is God real?' makes no more sense
than does the question-form 'Do material objects exist?'. It is
true that a man who rejects religious belief and does not believe
in God is not cut off from reason - is not thereby shown to be
irrational - as is the man who does not believe there are any
physical objects. Indeed, we would not know what to make of a
child's doubting the reality of physical objects, but we would
understand very well a child's not believing in God or an adult's
coming not to believe in God. The kind of unquestionable
propositions that Moore and Wittgenstein take to be bedrock
unquestionable propositions may, in their normal employments in
normal contexts, very well be propositions it really makes no
sense to question. They are framework beliefs. Whatever other
differences they may exhibit, they are propositions which are not
- or at least so these Wittgensteinians claim - testable
empirically and thus are, in that way, not grounded in experience
(7). There is no finding out whether they are true or false. The
fact, these Wittgensteinians claim, that the basic teachings of
religion cannot properly be called knowledge should cease to be
paradoxical, shocking or perplexing, when we reflect on this and
on the further fact that these various framework beliefs - certain
of them as we are - are still not bits of knowledge. Moreover,
that is not distinctive of religion and ideology, but is a
feature, as Wittgenstein shows, of many quite unproblematic

domains as well (8).   All language-games have their framework
propositions and, as they are something we cannot be mistaken
about or in any way test or establish, they are not bits of
knowledge.   Doubting, establishing, believing, finding out and
knowing are activities which make sense only within the confines
of language-games, and they require each other for any such single
activity to be possible.   But such contrastive conceptions cannot
be applied to the framework propositions themselves.   And while it
is perfectly true that cultural changes can and do bring about
changes in what we do and do not regard as reasonable, what
realism requires, Wittgenstein argues, is a recognition that we do
not have, and cannot come to have, a historical vantage point
which will tell us what, such historical contexts apart, is
'really reasonable' (9). (Indeed such talk may very well have no
coherent sense.) What we have in various areas are different and
often incommensurable beliefs which are, for many at least,
unshakable beliefs which regulate their lives.   But there is no
finding out which, if any of them, are really true.   There are,
such Wittgensteinians argue, no establishing 'philosophical
foundations' which show that some or all of them have a rational
underpinning.   Such rationalist hopes are utterly misguided (10).

To understand what we mean by 'God,' to grasp its role in the
stream of life, is to some to understand its role in such
religious activities as worship, prayer and the praise of God.
That is where we come to understand what it is that we believe in
when we believe in God.   That is where the experience of God will
have some reality, and it is in these surroundings that 'Thou art
God' has a clear sense.   There God becomes a reality in our lives,
and there it becomes clear to us that the existence of God is
neither a theoretical, nor a quasitheoretical, nor even some
metaphysical question.   We respond, if we are religious, to
religious talk, and on certain appropriate occasions some of us
even sing out 'God is our God above all other Gods.' Some
Wittgensteinians have even claimed that 'God exists,' in its
actual logical form (its depth grammar), is not something which
actually is, as it appears to be, in the indicative mood.   Most
definitely, such Wittgensteinians claim, it is not a statement of
fact or even a putative statement of fact.   'God,' they also
claim, is not a term concerning which it makes any sense at all to
look for its referent.   In Christian and Jewish language-games
'God is real' is a grammatical truth.

IV

These claims deserve a critical reception.   'God is unreal.
God is but a figment of our imaginations borne of our deepest
needs' are not deviant English sentences.   There are a number of
language-games in which such talk is quite at home.   But as
believers don't speak that way, it will be claimed that the above
skeptical utterances are not at home in religious language-games.

(But again, believers could act in a play and speak that way or write novels, as Dostoyevsky did, in which characters say such things.)

At least some believers understand such talk, and there are many ex-believers and doubting Thomases and people struggling in various ways with religious belief. In their struggles and in their expectable and understandable wrestlings with faith, such talk has a home. Questions about whether God is really a figment of our imagination quite naturally arise. Moreover, their typical contexts are not bizarre and metaphysical contexts in which we can ask whether physical objects are real or whether memory beliefs are ever reliable. In our lives, that is, they are, for believer and non-believer alike, not idling questions like 'Is time real?'.

It might be responded that it is necessary to recognize that, for a medieval man, asking whether 'God is real?' would be such an idling metaphysical question. Perhaps that is so - though that would have to be shown, for after all Machiavelli was a late medieval man - but, whatever we should say about the medievals, what is true in cultures such as ours is that such questions repeatedly arise in non-philosophical contexts where the engine is not idling. Why are they not in order in those contexts? What grounds have we for saying that they are not real doubts, or that they would never be asked by anyone who understood what he was asking? That some people - even that many people - do not question these propositions does not show they are 'unquestionable propositions.' That they are plainly not <u>just</u> theoretical questions does not show that they are not theoretical at all. Is it perhaps that changes over time and, in our culture, about what is taken to be reasonable and what is not have changed our responses to these questions and our attitudes toward worship, praise and prayer? But then we need to recognize just that, and consider what that involves and what philosophical significance it has.

It is indeed true that we need an understanding of God-talk to understand the sense of sentences such as 'I take my illness as a punishment,' 'Your sins are forgiven,' 'God is merciful to sinners,' and 'He has experienced God's mercy,' but we also need, to understand them properly, to see how they fit into a system. (We can speak of a 'system of salvation' and we need not think of it as a theoretical system.) But none of this precludes or makes unnecessary asking about the referent (alleged referent) of 'God.' Granted 'God' does not stand for an object among objects, but still, what does 'God' stand for? None of the above has shown that to be a pseudo-question.

V

Wittgensteinians - as is most evident in the work of Winch, Dilman and Phillips - try very hard to avoid facing that issue. Indeed they struggle to show that in reality there is no such issue at all (11). I have tried to expose the nerve of some of the issues here, and to maintain against them that there appears at least to be a real issue here.

Wittgensteinians will contend that language-games and forms of life are neither well-founded nor ill-founded. They are just there, like our lives. Our understanding of them and assurance concerning them is shown by the way we go on - by how we employ them - whether we claim, in our philosophical moments, to understand them or not. There is no showing that the evaluative conceptions and norms, including the norms of reasonability embedded in them, require a justification, a foundation or even an explanation. Indeed, if they are right, the first two are impossible and even the third (i.e., that they require explanation) may be impossible as well, but impossible or not, such things, they claim, are unnecessary. The urge to attempt such justifications and explanations is very deep - as deep as the very subject that has traditionally been called 'philosophy.' But Wittgenstein schools us to resist this urge. If he is near to the mark, reason - the use by human beings of the various canons of rationality - requires that we resist it. Such general inquiries about religion and reality are senseless. There neither is nor can be a <u>philosophical</u> underpinning of religion or anything else. But such <u>philosophical</u> foundationalism is not needed. It is not, these Wittgensteinian Fideists claim, something the loss of which undermines our capacity to make sense of our lives. Bad philosophy gives us the illusion that religion requires such a foundation and sometimes succeeds in so infiltrating religious conceptions that they do come to have incoherent elements which should not be accepted. Good philosophy will help us spot and excise those nonsensical, metaphysical elements. But when purified of such extraneous metaphysical elements, religious belief is both foundationaless and not in the slightest need of foundations or some philosophical justification.

I do not intend here to rise to the fundamental metaphilosophical issues raised by this Wittgensteinian rejection of the search for 'philosophical foundations.' Such a way of viewing things is plainly less popular now than when Wittgenstein and some of his followers first pressed it home. Yet it seems to me that philosophers have not so much answered it, or shown it to be a pointless lament, as simply to have ignored it. I think that this is a mistake, and that any philosophical practice that survives taking this challenge seriously will look very different indeed from the practices that went before it.

However, I don't want to consider that grand issue here, but only to face some of its implications for religion, if one takes to heart Wittgenstein's critique of the pretensions of philosophy. I agree that religion can have no such philosophical or metaphysical foundations. I do not even have a tolerably clear sense of what it means to say that there is some <u>distinctive philosophical</u> knowledge that would give us 'the true grounds' of religious belief. I am no more concerned than are the

Wittgensteinians to defend such a metaphysical religiosity, and I am not concerned to replace it with some distinctive atheological 'philosophical knowledge.'

However, our perplexities and difficulties about God and religion are not just in a second-order context where the engine is idling. Most of them are not like perplexities about how we can know whether there is an external world, or whether induction is justified, or whether our memory beliefs are ever reliable. It is not just the talk about God-talk that perplexes us, but certain central bits of the first-order talk itself. People with a common culture and a common set of language-games are very much at odds over whether we can know or justifiably believe that there is a God. This issue can be, and often is, linked for some with an intense desire to believe in God or, for that matter (though much less frequently), not to believe in God. It is common ground between myself and Wittgensteinian Fideists that we do not think that there is any metaphysical Santa Claus that is going to provide us with answers here, to wit with some distinctively 'metaphysical knowledge' which will assure us that there is or is not, must or cannot be, that putative reality for which 'God' is the English term.

Using their own procedures, procedures I take to be perfectly proper, I started by looking at religious language-games we all can play, and concerning which we at least have a knowledge by wont. When we look at certain religious language-games and - indeed from inside them - put questions which are perfectly natural, questions that plain people ask, and ask without suffering from metaphysical hunger, we will see that perplexities arise about to whom or to what we could be praying, supplicating or even denying when we talk in this manner. Where 'God' is construed nonanthropomorphically, as we must construe 'God' if our conception is not to betray our belief as a belief in a superstition, it appears at least to be the case that we do not understand who or what it is we believe in when we speak of believing in God. It is not just that we do not understand these matters very well - that is certainly to be expected and is quite tolerable - but that we are utterly at sea here.

Such considerations make skepticism about the reality of such a conception very real indeed. And that very skepticism - as Dostoyevsky teaches us - can even come from someone who has a genuine need or at least a desire to believe. Such skepticism is common enough and, if I am near to my mark, could be well-founded, even in complete innocence of, or in utter irony about, philosophical foundations for or against religious belief.

27

NOTES

1. Ludwig Wittgenstein, On Certainty, translated by Denis Paul
and G. E. M. Anscombe (Oxford: Basil Blackwell, 1969) and Norman
Malcolm, "The Groundlessness of Belief," in Reason and Religion,
ed. Stuart C. Brown (Ithaca, New York: Cornell University Press,
1977), pp. 143-157 and 186-190.

2. Wittgenstein in On Certainty and again in a somewhat different
way in his Philosophical Investigations. See Rush Rhees, Without
Answers (London: Routledge and Kegan Paul, 1969); the article
cited in the previous footnote from Malcolm; D. Z. Phillips, The
Concept of Prayer (London: Routledge and Kegan Paul, 1965), Death
and immortality (New York: St. Martin's Press, 1979), Faith and
Philosophical Enquiry (London: Routledge and Kegan Paul, 1970),
and Religion Without Explanation (Oxford: Basil Blackwell, 1976);
Ilham Dilman, "Wisdom's Philosophy of Religion," Canadian Journal
of Philosophy, Vol. V, No. 4 (December, 1975); and "Wittgenstein
On the Soul," in Understanding Wittgenstein, ed. G. Vesey (London:
MacMillan, 1974).

3. In addition to the above references, note as well Peter Winch,
"Understanding a Primitive Society," in Bryan R. Wilson (ed.),
Rationality (Oxford: Basil Blackwell, 1970) and "Meaning and
Religious Language," in Reason and Religion, ed. Stuart C. Brown.

4. See the above references to Phillips and Winch and, most
centrally, Wittgenstein, On Certainty. I discuss further facets
of this in my "Reasonable Belief Without Justification," in Body
Mind and Method: Essays in Honor of Virgil C. Aldrich
(Dordrecht-Holland: D., Reidel, 1979), Donald Gustafson and Bangs
L. Tapscott (eds.).

5. Most of the above references are pertinent here, but note as
well D. Z. Phillips, "Philosophers, Religion and Conceptual
Change," in The Challenge of Religion Today, ed. John King-Farlow
(New York: Neale Watson Academic Publications, 1976), pp. 190-200.

6. See my Contemporary Critiques of Religion (New York: Herder
and Herder, 1971) and my Scepticism (New York: St. Martin's,
1973), and see A.G.N. Flew's God and Philosophy (London:
Hutchinson, 1966) and A.G.N. Flew's The Presumption of Atheism
(New York: Barnes and Noble, 1976).

7. Norman Malcolm, op. cit.

8. Ludwig Wittgenstein, On Certainty, and G. H. von Wright,
"Wittgenstein On Certainty," in Problems in the Theory of
Knowledge, ed. G. H. von Wright (The Hague: Martinus Nijhoff,
1972), pp. 47-60.

9. Ludwig Wittgenstein, On Certainty, pp. 43 and 80.

10. Again, On Certainty seems to me a crucial reference here. See also Stanley Cavell, Must We Mean What We Say? (New York: Charles Schribner's Sons, 1969).

11. Such accounts have been powerfully criticized by Robert C. Coburn, "Animadversions on a Wittgensteinian Apologetic," Perkins Journal (Spring, 1971), pp. 25-36, and by Michael Durrant, "Is the Justification of Religious Belief a Possible Enterprise?", Religious Studies, Vol. 9 (1971), pp. 449-454 and in his "Some Comments on 'Meaning and Religious Language'," in Reason and Religion, ed. Stuart C. Brown.

Reprinted with permission from Frederick J. Crosson, ed., The Antonomy of Religious Belief: A Critical Inquiry (Notre Dame: University of Notre Dame Press, 1981), pp. 93-107.

Religious Experience as a Ground of Religious Belief
William P. Alston

I

The question I wish to consider is whether religious experience can provide any ground or basis for religious belief, whether it can serve to justify religious belief, or make it rational. This paper will differ from many others in the literature by virtue of looking at this question in the light of basic epistemological issues. Throughout we will be comparing the epistemology of religious experience with the epistemology of sense experience.

First we must distinguish between experience directly providing justification for a belief and indirectly providing justification. It indirectly provides justification for belief B1 when it provides justification for some other beliefs, which in turn provide justification for B1. Thus I have learned indirectly from experience that Beaujolais wine is fruity, because I have learned from experience that this, that, and the other bottle of Beaujolais is fruity, and these propositions support the generalization. Experience will directly justify a belief when the justification does not go through other beliefs in this way. There are quite different views as to just how experience can directly provide justification, and some epistemologists deny that it can happen at all. In this paper I shall think of direct experiential justification in terms of the subject's being justified, by virtue of having the experience, in taking what he is experiencing to be so-and-so. Thus if I am justified, by virtue of having the visual experiences I am now having, in supposing what I am experiencing to be a typewriter situated directly in front of me, then the belief that there is a typewriter directly in front of me is directly justified by that experience. Less controversially, I may be directly justified by my experience in taking it that I feel upset.

On the explanation just given, any justification by reasons where the chain of reasons will eventually lead to beliefs justified directly by experience, will count as indirect experiential justification. I don't really want to cast the net that wide, but for our purposes it will not be necessary to draw a precise line. Let's just say that under the heading of indirect justification by experience we will restrict ourselves to cases in which direct experiential justification comes into the picture not very far back.

We find claims to both direct and indirect justification of religious beliefs by religious experience. Where someone believes that her new way of relating herself to the world after her conversion is to be explained by the Holy Spirit imparting super-natural graces to her, she supposes her belief that the Holy Spirit imparts graces to her to be indirectly justified by her experience. What she directly learns from experience is that she sees and reacts to things differently; this is then taken as a reason for supposing that the Holy Spirit is imparting graces to her. When, on the other hand, one takes himself to be experiencing the presence of God, he thinks that his experience justifies him in supposing that God is what he is experiencing. Thus he supposes himself to be directly justified by his experience in believing God to be present to him.

No doubt this distinction is often difficult to draw, especially with respect to religious experience. Nevertheless there is a real distinction to be drawn here. A good way to get at the distinction is this. Suppose the subject was asked: "Just what were you aware of?", where it is clear that this asks for a specification of the object of awareness (consciousness) rather than how one is interpreting it or explaining it, or what suppositions one is forming about it. Then if the subject answers that question by saying "the presence of God" or "God sustaining my being," rather than, e.g., "a profound sense of peace," or "a feeling of being filled with power," we may say that the subject takes himself to directly experience the presence of God, and to be directly justified by his experience in believing that God is present to him. If he answers in the second way, then he is, at most, indirectly justified by his experience in supposing God to be present to him. The crucial difference lies in what the subject takes to be the most basic way of specifying what he was experiencing, what he was aware of. That is, this is what is crucial to what he takes himself to be directly justified in believing on the basis of experience. Whether he is so justified is a further question.

In this paper I am going to confine myself to the question of whether religious experience can provide direct justification for religious belief. This has some implications for the class of experiences we shall be considering. In the widest sense 'religious experience' ranges over any experiences one has in connection with one's religious life, including any joys, fears, longings, or whatever one has in a religious context. But here I am concerned with experiences that could be taken to directly justify religious beliefs. Given the above explanation of that notion, this means that we are confining ourselves to experiences the subject takes to involve a direct awareness of what the religious belief is about. In order to further focus the discussion, let's confine ourselves to beliefs to the effect that God, as conceived in theistic religions, is doing something that is directed to the subject of the experience - that God is speaking to him, comforting him, strengthening him, enlightening him, giving him courage, guiding him, pouring out His love or joy into him, sustaining him in being, or just being present to him. Call these "M-beliefs" ('M' for 'manifestation'). I want to focus on M-beliefs because they seem the best candidates for theistic beliefs that are directly justified by experience. Relatively abstract theological beliefs in the trinity, the incarnation, and the details of the divine nature would seem to be no more susceptible of direct justification by experience than are high-level scientific theories. Just as the public facts we can glean directly from sense experience consist, at most, in facts about the nature and situation of particular physical objects in the immediate vicinity, so it would seem that the theological facts I could learn directly from religious experience would consist, at most, in facts about how God impinges on my life. And, to continue the analogy, just as we would never reach any knowledge of "theoretical scientific facts" unless we had access to humble facts about particular middle-sized objects in the immediate vicinity, so it may be contended that we would never learn anything about the existence and nature and plans of God unless we could be aware of His operations in my life-space.

Finally, I will confine myself to religious experiences enjoyed by ordinary devout believers who have not undertaken a major contemplative or ascetic discipline, and who have not sacrificed all else to the attainment of an immediate vision of God. This means that I sacrifice the most obvious continuity with the bulk of the philosophical literature on the epistemology of religious experience, which concentrates, much too narrowly, on highly developed mystical experience. It is not surprising that so splashy and so easily demarcated a phenomenon as classical mystical experience should have attracted so much attention, but such experience, because of the extreme immediacy and ineffability allegedly involved, poses very special problems not generated by its humbler relatives; and the obsession with mystical experience has led to a serious neglect of the epistemology of the person in the pew.

II

Let's call the view that religious experience can directly justify M-beliefs "religious empiricism." Religious empiricism is compatible with a wide variety of views as to the place of religious experience in a complete epistemology of religious belief. For example, it is compatible both with the view that experience merely serves to confirm or disconfirm other independent, and perhaps more basic, sources of justification, and with the view that the experiential justification of M-beliefs is basic to the whole edifice of religious belief. I will not be going into these wider questions in this essay.

What is our highest reasonable aspiration for being directly justified by experience? Being justified no matter what else is the case? A brief consideration of sense perception would suggest a negative answer. I may be justified in believing that there is a tree in front of me by virtue of the fact that I am currently having a certain kind of sense experience, but this will be true only in "favorable circumstances." If I am confronted with a complicated arrangement of mirrors, I may not be justified in believing that there is an oak tree in front of me, even though it looks for all the world as if there is. Again, it may look for all the world as if water is running uphill, but the general improbability of this greatly diminishes the justification the corresponding belief receives from that experience. What this shows is that the justification provided by one's sense experience is only prima facie or defeasible. It is inherently liable to be overridden, diminished, or canceled by stronger considerations to the contrary.

It would seem that direct experiential justification for M-beliefs is also, at most, prima facie. Beliefs about the nature and ways of God are often used to override M-beliefs, particularly beliefs concerning communications from God. If I report that God told me to kill all Wittgensteinians, fellow Christians will, no doubt, dismiss the report on the grounds that God wouldn't give me any such injunction as that. I shall take it that both sensory experience and religious experience provide, at most, prima facie justification.

Religious empiricism consists of a general principle of justification, a principle that specifies conditions under which beliefs of a certain sort are prima facie justified. Let's formulate the principle as follows.

> I. An M-belief is prima facie justified if it arises from a an experience that seems to the subject to be an experience of what is believed. (Call the underlined condition 'C'.)

I. implies, e.g., that if I come to believe that God is sustaining me in being because I seem to experience myself being sustained in being by God, then that belief is prima facie justified. In considering whether I. is true, acceptable, rational, or whatever, we shall have to go on some assumptions, explicit or implicit, as to what it is for a belief to be justified. Let's be explicit about this.

III

First, the justification about which we are asking is an "epistemic" rather that a "moral" or "prudential" justification. What makes a justification epistemic? As the name implies, it has something to do with knowledge, or more broadly, with the aim at attaining truth and avoiding falsity. At a first approximation, I am justified in believing that p when, from the point of view of that aim, there is something O.K., all right, to be approved, about the fact that I believe that $\underline{p}$. But when we come to spell this out further, we find that a fundamental distinction must be drawn between two different ways of being in an epistemically commendable position.

On the one hand there is what we may call a "normative" concept of epistemic justification (Jn), "normative" because it has to do with how we stand vis-a-vis norms that specify our intellectual obligations, obligations that attach to one $\underline{qua}$ truth seeker. Stated most generally, to be Jn in believing that $\underline{p}$ consists in not having violated one's intellectual obligations in believing that $\underline{p}$. We have to say "not having violated" rather than "having fulfilled" because in all normative spheres, being justified is a negative status; it amounts to one's behavior not being in violation of the norms. For example, to say that my expenditures on the trip were justified is not to say that I was obliged to make those expenditures (e.g., for taxis), but only that it was all right for me to do so, that in doing so I was not in violation of any relevant rules or regulations. If belief is under voluntary control, we may think of intellectual obligations as attaching directly to believing, as most advocates of a normative conception do. Thus one might be obliged to refrain from believing in the absence of adequate evidence. But if, as seems obvious to me, belief is not under voluntary control, obligations cannot attach directly to believing. However, I do have voluntary control over moves that can influence a particular belief formation, e.g., looking for more evidence, and moves that can affect my belief-forming habits or tendencies, e.g., training myself to be more critical of testimony. This suggests that we might think of the relevant normative principles as governing what we can do voluntarily to influence our beliefs. One will be doing one's intellectual duty if one engages in such belief-influencing activities as the norms require. We can then think of being-in-the-clear, normatively, in believing as derivative from that, as consisting, roughly, in the fact that the belief does not stem from violations of such intellectual obligations. It would be like the way in which one is or isn't to blame for other conditions or processes that are not themselves under voluntary control. I am subject to reproach for being overweight (being irritable, being in poor health, being without friends) only if the condition is in some way due to my own past failures to do what I should to limit my intake or to exercise or whatever. If I would still be overweight even if I had done everything I could and should have done about it, then I can hardly be blamed for it. Similarly, we may say that I am subject to reproach for believing that $\underline{p}$ only if there are things I could and should have done, such that if I had done them I would not now be believing that $\underline{p}$. If that is the case I am normatively unjustified in that belief. If that is not the case, if my believing that $\underline{p}$ does not depend on violation of intellectual obligations, then I am normatively justified, Jn, in believing that $\underline{p}$. I will be restricting myself to this "involuntaristic" version of Jn, the one that does not assume belief to be under direct voluntary control.

Some epistemologists, on the other hand, use the term 'justified' in such a way that it has to do not with how the subject stands vis-a-vis obligations, but rather with the strength of her epistemic position in believing that p, with how likely it is that a belief of that sort acquired or held in that way is true. In what ways can one's "position" in believing that p be a strong one, vis-a-vis the aim at truth? How can the way in which one believes that p be "truth-conducive"? For one thing, p might be well-supported by reasons that one has, by other things one knows or is justified in believing. I. could not be true on this "reasonableness" account of justification, just as no other claim to direct justification by experience could be. For to say that a belief is directly supported by experience is to say that, given the appropriate experience (plus the absence of defeaters, if that is needed), the belief is justified whether or not the subject has adequate reasons for the belief. A less ad hoc reason for dismissing this understanding of justification is that it ignores the way in which the belief originated and/or is sustained; on the "reasonableness" conception one might have adequate reasons for a belief, whatever produces or sustains the belief. But any set of conditions that leaves open the possibility that a belief arose as a sheer guess, or on the basis of wishful thinking, cannot be sufficient for epistemic justification.

There is a "truth-conduciveness" conception of justification that is more interesting for our purposes. This is the "reliability" conception, according to which a belief is justified iff it arose from a process of belief formation and/or sustenance that is a generally reliable one, that can be generally relied on to produce true beliefs (1). This is the most obvious way in which a subject can believe that p in a way that is generally truth-conducive. Where the belief is due to a process that is a generally reliable one, it is not just a matter of hitting the mark in this particular instance. Let us dub this "reliability" conception of justification 'Jr'. In discussing I., I will restrict myself to Jr and Jn.

To underscore the difference between Jn and Jr, let's consider some cases in which a practice is justified in the one sense but not in the other. Consider a naive member of an isolated primitive tribe who, along with his fellows, unhesitatingly accepts the traditions of the tribe. That is, he engages in the practice of believing p wherever the traditions of the tribe, as recited by the elders, include the assertion that p. He is normatively justified in doing so, for he has no reason whatsoever to doubt these traditions. Everyone he knows accepts them without question, and they do not conflict with anything else he believes. And yet, let us suppose, this is in fact not a reliable procedure of belief formation, and so he is not justified in the Jr sense. Conversely, a procedure may be in fact reliable, though I have strong reasons for regarding it as unreliable and so would not be normatively justified in engaging in it; to do so would be to ignore those reasons and so would be a violation of an intellectual obligation. Suppose that I have been presented with overwhelming, though spurious, evidence that for about half the time over the last ten years I have, without realizing it, been in a physiological laboratory where my sensory experience was artificially produced. In this case I have strong reasons for supposing that I cannot tell at a given moment whether I am engaging in normal perception or not; and so I have strong reasons for regarding my perceptual belief-forming processes as unreliable. Nevertheless they are as reliable as any normal person's.

IV

If I. is interpreted in terms of Jr, then the question of its truth is just the question of whether the "epistemic practice" (2), as we might say, of forming M-beliefs on the basis of religious experience is a generally reliable one. I will consider in due time what can be said on this score. But first, let's see what the issue amounts to if I. is understood in terms of Jn.

Remember that being Jn in believing that p hangs on whether that belief depends on some failure to carry out intellectual obligations. But here we are talking not about the justification of a particular belief; we are considering whether all M-beliefs that satisfy condition C are justified. If that is the case, then, understanding justification as Jn, no M-belief that satisfies C depends on any failure of intellectual obligation. The question of whether all M-beliefs that satisfy C are Jn is just the question of whether the satisfaction of C by an M-belief insures that the belief does not stem from a failure to carry out intellectual obligations.

Whether this is so is going to depend, inter alia, on what intellectual obligations we have. Let's take it that our most fundamental aim as intellectual beings is to believe the true and to avoid believing the false. Now if belief were under voluntary control, that would mean that our most fundamental obligation would be, for each proposition p we consider, to believe that p iff it is true, or, more realistically, to believe that p iff we have sufficient reason to suppose it to be true. But since we are not taking belief to be under voluntary control, our intellectual obligations will have to be thought of as applying to things that we can do voluntarily to affect our belief-forming practices, what we are calling "epistemic practices." Keeping in mind the fundamental aim at truth and the avoidance of falsity, we can then say that our basic intellectual obligation is to try to make our epistemic practice as reliable as possible, as well-designed as possible to produce true and only true beliefs (3).

Because our belief-forming processes are only imperfectly under our (indirect) control, the obligation had to be stated in terms of <u>trying</u> to bring it about that we engage only in reliable practices. To avoid tedious circumlocutions I shall henceforth make the simplifying assumption that belief-forming processes are wholly within our (indirect) control. Thus we can speak of being obliged to restrict ourselves to reliable practices, rather than of being obliged to <u>try</u> to so restrict ourselves (4). This gives us the following formulation of our basic intellectual obligation.

> II. One is obliged to refrain from engaging in
> an epistemic practice <u>iff</u> it is reliable (5).

However, to put it this way overestimates our capacity to determine the reliability of practices. If we could always or usually ascertain reliability on inspection, II. would be a satisfactory formulation. But in fact the most we have, all too often, are reasons that are far from conclusive. This suggests that the condition for our being obliged to refrain should be couched in terms of reasons we have that bear on unreliability, rather than in terms of unreliability itself. But when we set out to make this revision we find that there are two candidates for a sufficient condition for an obligation to refrain. On the one hand there are adequate reasons for taking a practice, P, to be unreliable; and on the other hand there is the lack of adequate reasons for taking P to be reliable. Everyone who has gone along with the argument up to this point will agree that the former generates an intellectual obligation to refrain; if that doesn't, nothing does. But there will be controversy over the latter. Suppose that I do actually engage in practice P, or have a considerable tendency to do so. And suppose that I have sufficient reasons neither for a judgment of reliability nor for a judgment of unreliability. Am I obliged to refrain (remembering our assumption of effective control)? This issue is reminiscent of the famous Clifford-James confrontation over the ethics of belief. There it was the question of whether one is justified in believing only when in possession of adequate reasons for the proposition believed, or whether the mere absence of adequate reasons for the contradictory entitles one to believe. Are beliefs to be held guilty until proved innocent, or innocent until proved guilty? We are now considering a precisely parallel issue concerning epistemic practices. Those who take the hard, Cliffordian line hold that one is obliged to refrain unless one has adequate reasons for reliability; while the partisans of the more permissive, Jamesian line hold that one is obliged to refrain only if one has adequate reasons for unreliability. They agree that one is obliged to refrain where one has adequate reasons for unreliability, and they agree that one is not so obliged where one has adequate reasons for reliability. But they disagree over the case in which one has adequate reasons for neither.

The Jamesian position might be supported by bringing in our need to guide our behavior by our beliefs. Suppose that we have adequate reasons for the reliability of none, or very few, epistemic practices. (The further course of this paper will indicate that this is a live possibility.) In that case, the stricter line would have us form no, or very few, beliefs; and that is hardly a defensible position. But it is not my aim in this paper to settle this issue. Instead I want to recognize both these positions, and consider the application of each to our central problem concerning religious empiricism. Let's formulate each principle of obligation as follows. The stricter one will read:

> III. One is obliged to refrain from engaging in an epistemic practice _iff_ it is not the case that one has adequate reasons for taking that practice to be reliable.

And the more permissive one will read:

> IV. One is obliged to refrain from engaging in an epistemic practice _iff_ one has adequate reasons for taking that epistemic practice to be unreliable (6).

Now let's apply all this to the question of the truth of I. on a Jn construal. Let's use the term 'Jns' for Jn with the strong principle of obligation, III., and the term 'Jnw' for Jn with the weaker principle of obligation, IV. Now we can say that M-beliefs that satisfy C are Jns provided there are adequate reasons for the reliability of the practice of forming M-beliefs in the presence of C. (Call this practice 'RE', for 'religious experience.') For if there are such reasons then one has not violated any intellectual obligations in engaging in RE, and so beliefs formed from that practice are Jn. Whereas M-beliefs that satisfy C are Jnw, provided that there are no adequate reasons for the unreliability of RE. For in that case one has not violated IV. in engaging in RE, and so beliefs formed by RE are Jn. Thus the question of whether M-beliefs that satisfy C are Jn boils down to the question of whether there are adequate reasons for the reliability or for the unreliability of RE.

We have just been making an additional idealization. Whether a given person is Jn in believing that p does not depend on what reasons there are (in the abstract, in general) for or against the reliability of the appropriate practice; it depends on what reasons that person has. And this can, and will, vary a great deal from person to person. But in this paper we are not interested in individual variations. We want to know whether one can be justified by one's experience in holding an M-belief; we want to know whether there are conditions, satisfiable currently by actual human beings, under which one would be so justified. In order to bypass individual variation we shall be thinking in terms of an idealized subject that is _au courant_ with whatever relevant reasons are available to a reasonably educated, intelligent, and reflective person today. With that idealization the question of

Jn will hang on what reasons are available.

Hearkening back to Jr, we remember that whether M-beliefs that satisfy C are Jr depends on whether RE is reliable. But in discussing that issue there is nothing for us to do except to determine what reasons there are for and against the reliability of RE. It is not as if it is self-evident, or otherwise immediately knowable, that RE is or is not reliable. But that is just what we have to consider to determine whether I. is true on a Jn construal. So, whatever concept of justification we pick, the issue will hang on what reasons there are for the reliability or unreliability of RE.

V

I want to set my discussion of reasons for or against the reliability of RE in the context of a general discussion of the evaluation of epistemic practices. For only in that way can we assess the significance of the results we will obtain for the restricted question of RE.

First, let's distinguish between what we may call practices of belief creation (C-practices) and practices of belief transformation (T-practices). A C-practice "creates" beliefs out of something other than beliefs, while T-practices produce new beliefs from old beliefs (perhaps along with other conditions) (7). A C-practice, so to say, creates beliefs out of non-doxastic materials, while a T-practice might be thought of as simply transforming an initial set of beliefs into other beliefs with different contents. (If this picture gives you trouble, just take the terms as arbitrary labels.) RE is a C-practice, since the operative condition involves a certain kind of experience and the absence of defeaters; it does not include other beliefs. More generally, any practice of forming beliefs "directly" from experience will count as a C-practice.

To simplify and focus the discussion I will restrict myself to C-practices. In particular I will concentrate on comparing the epistemic status of RE with a much more thoroughly explored C-practice, that of forming beliefs about the immediate physical environment on the basis of sense experience. Let's call such a practice 'PP' (for 'perceptual practice'). PP gives rise to the same epistemological questions as RE. We may ask whether a perceptual belief about the immediate environment (P-belief), e.g., the belief that there is a maple tree in front of me, is justified by virtue of arising from a certain kind of sense-experience. And again our highest reasonable aspiration will be a prima facie justification. The principle of justification for P-beliefs, parallel to I. for M-beliefs, will be:

> V. A P-belief is prima facie justified if it arises from a sense experience that seems to the subject to present the fact believed.

40

(Call the underlined condition 'D'.)

And in deciding whether V. is true, on various concepts of justification, we will, by the line of reasoning just sketched for I., be driven back to parallel problems as to what reasons there are for the reliability or unreliability of PP. Thus the comparison of the epistemic statuses of RE and PP will boil down to an investigation of the reasons for the reliability or unreliability of the two practices (8).

VI

Let's begin with reasons for the reliability of PP, and first let's note a reason for pessimism about our chances. We may distinguish between "basic" and "derived" epistemic practices. As far as C-practices are concerned, the gut idea of a basic practice is that it is one that constitutes our basic access to its subject-matter, so that any other access presupposes it. Of course, if we put it that way we would seem to be presupposing the validity of the practice in question, so let's put it negatively. A C-practice, P, is basic provided there is no other practice that yields beliefs about its subject-matter and which is such that its reliability is independent of the reliability of P. It would seem that PP is basic in this sense. Any other way of finding out about the physical world presupposes the reliability of PP. The use of instruments like thermometers, e.g., presupposes the reliability of PP, both because we have to use PP to get the thermometer reading and because our confidence in those readings is ultimately based on data obtained by PP.

Here is why this is a reason for pessimism. We are unable to marshall the most direct conceivable reasons for the reliability of PP, viz., a comparison of its deliverances with the facts in question. For we would have to ascertain those facts either by PP itself or some other practice. And in either case, since PP is basic, we would be presupposing the reliability of PP and the reasoning would be circular.

Before proceeding further we should specify the kind of circularity just alluded to. It is not logical circularity. Even if one uses PP itself to provide reasons for the claim that PP is reliable, that claim does not itself appear among the premises of one's argument. For example, suppose that I argue for the reliability of PP by citing the fact that by engaging in PP we are enabled to gain some considerable success in predicting the future course of events. Here we use PP, of course, to ascertain that this is the case. We tell what people predict by listening to what they say and reading what they write. And we tell whether things come out as they predict by taking a look or a listen. But the claim of the reliability of PP does not appear among our premises. Those premises just contain claims of predictive success. Then where is the circularity? It comes in the fact that in supposing ourselves entitled to those premises we are

relying (in practice) on the reliability of PP. The reliability
of PP is a presupposition of our adducing those premises (9).
Let's term this mode of circularity "epistemic circularity." We
may say that an argument is epistemically circular <u>iff</u> the
conclusion is assumed (at least in practice) by the arguer in
supposing himself to <u>know</u>, or to be <u>justified</u> in believing, the
premises.

It is not obvious that epistemic circularity is a fatal flaw
in an argument (10). But if epistemic circularity is to be
allowed, then it will be too easy to mount an acceptable argument
for the reliability of <u>any</u> C-practice. We simply compare the
deliverances of that practice with the facts, as determined by
that practice. The practice being tested will always score 100%.
Moreover, epistemically circular arguments are dialectically
impotent in a context in which the reliability of a practice is in
question. If I doubt that P is reliable, or if I am just trying
to determine whether there are any reasons for supposing it to be,
I am unlikely to be impressed with the point that it can be shown
to be reliable if we use <u>it</u> to produce the premises. In this
paper we are examining the reliability of RE in a context in which
its reliability is not taken for granted. And we want, by
comparison, to see what could be done to show the reliability of
PP in a context in which that was not taken for granted.
Therefore we shall disallow epistemically circular arguments.
From now on 'circular' is to be read 'epistemically circular.'

Since we are unable, without circularity, to check the
testimony of PP against the facts attested to, how could we
establish its reliability? Well, there have been a number of
ingenious attempts to use other practices, usually purely rational
ones, to establish facts that will provide support for taking PP
to be reliable. Thus Descartes appealed to the veracity and
benevolence of God, which he took himself to have established <u>a
priori</u>. Wittgenstein, Strawson, and others have employed
transcendental arguments to the effect that the reliability of PP
is a necessary condition of having a conception of oneself or
attributing states of consciousness to oneself or using a language
(11). More recently Michael Slote and Richard Brandt have argued
on methodological grounds that relying on PP is the most rational
move to make. Some of these arguments exhibit epistemic
circularity, albeit in a less blatant form than, e.g., the appeal
to predictive success. Others suffer from a variety of other
defects. I believe that none of them succeed, and I see little
hope that others will do better. If I had a general argument for
the impossibility of success I would certainly unveil it at this
point, but in the absence of such an argument my position can be
supported only by unmasking each pretender in turn. Obviously I
have no time for that here; I am forced to simply assume that
there are no adequate non-circular reasons for the reliability of
PP. Given that assumption, it follows that our P-beliefs are not
Jns by sense-experience. And though they <u>may</u> be Jr, we lack
sufficient positive reason for supposing them to be.

What about reasons for the unreliability of PP? Here there will be little controversy. Except for those who, like Parmenides and Bradley, have argued that there are ineradicable inconsistencies in the conceptual scheme involved in PP, philosophers have not supposed that we can show that sense perception is an unreliable guide to our immediate surroundings. Sceptics about sense perception have generally confined themselves to arguing that we can't show that sense perception is reliable; i.e., they have argued that PP is not Jns. I shall assume without further argument that we do not have adequate reasons for taking PP to be unreliable, and hence that our P-beliefs are Jnw by sense-experience.

Thus it would seem that Jnw is the most we have sufficient reason to attribute to P-beliefs, on the basis of sense-experience. In other words, we have adequate reason to take V. to be true only on the Jnw interpretation. Now let's turn to M-beliefs and begin there, too, by asking whether we have adequate reasons for the reliability of RE.

VII

The first thing to ask in this connection is whether RE is a basic C-practice. Many would suppose that it is not. We may neutralize partisans of revelation as an independent source of knowledge about God by maintaining that revelation must be received through the experience of revelatees, so that this is just a special form of RE. But there still remains the claim that we can gain knowledge of God by reasoning from premises that make no appeal to RE. And even if RE is basic, there could still be parallels to the attempts to show PP to be reliable. Since this is something else I will not have time to go into, I shall just assume that a thorough examination would reveal that here too there are no adequate non-circular reasons for the reliability of RE, and hence that M-beliefs are not Jns by experience. And once more, though they may be Jr, we have no sufficient positive reason for supposing them to be.

This brings us once more to Jnw. If M-beliefs are Jnw, then their epistemic status is quite parallel to that of P-beliefs. And they will be, provided that there are no adequate reasons for regarding RE as unreliable. Are there such reasons? What might they be?

First, we can have the most direct and unquestionably relevant reason for regarding an epistemic practice as unreliable if we have ascertained that its outputs are generally incorrect, or not generally correct. Now to the extent that RE yields beliefs about matters that we also have some other, perhaps more favored way of discovering, its unreliability could be shown in this way. Perhaps something like this is involved when fundamentalist Christians take it on the "inward testimony of the Holy Spirit" that the Bible is the word of God and then suppose

43

that in the Bible God is telling us about the physical history and
constitution of the universe. However, one who engages in RE need
not get involved in anything like that. I shall restrict the
discussion to a kind of RE that only yields beliefs about God, His
nature and His doings, the truth or falsity of which are not
assessable on empirical or scientific grounds.

That still leaves the possibility that we might establish
conclusions by philosophical reasoning that contradict all or many
of the products of RE. For example, we might demonstrate the
non-existence of God. Or, contrariwise, we might be able to show
that God's nature is such that He couldn't be doing what He is
frequently represented in RE as doing. Finally, we might be able
to show that RE yields a system of belief that is ineradicably
internally inconsistent. (I am not speaking of isolated and
remediable inconsistencies that continually pop up in every area
of thought and experience.) I don't believe that we are able to
bring off any of this, but again I won't have time to argue the
point (12). Instead I will pass on to some other putative grounds
for unreliability, where the considerations alleged are relatively
uncontroversial; it is their relevance to the question of
reliablity that is dubious.

I believe that many people are inclined to take RE to be
discredited by certain ways in which it differs from PP, by the
lack of certain salient features of PP. These include the
following.

1. Within PP there are standard ways of checking the accuracy of
any particular perceptual belief.

2. By engaging in PP we can discover regularities in the behavior
of the objects putatively observed, and on this basis we can, to a
certain extent, effectively predict the course of events.

3. Capacity for PP, and practice of it, is found universally
among normal adult human beings.

4. All normal adult human beings, whatever their culture, use
basically the same conceptual scheme in objectifying their sense
experience.

It is the first of these features that has been most often
invoked in this connection by twentieth-century philosophers.
Nevertheless it is just a special case of 2. Our standard
checking procedures in PP presuppose that we know a good deal
about the ways in which things can be expected to behave in the
physical world. Consider the appeal to other observers. Suppose
I think I see a fir tree across the street from my house. What
would count as intersubjective corroboration? Not any report of
seeing a fir tree. If someone reports seeing a fir tree in Nepal,
that will not tend to show that there is a fir tree across from my
house. Nor will the failure of someone in Nepal, or across town,

to see a fir tree have any tendency to disconfirm my report. Nor if a blind man stands just where I was standing and fails to see a fir tree, would that disconfirm my report. The point is, of course, that only observers that satisfy certain conditions as to location, condition, state of the environment, etc., can qualify as either confirming or disconfirming my report. And how do we know what conditions to specify? We do it in the light of presumed regularities in the interaction of physical objects and sentient subjects. Persons in certain circumstances, and only in those circumstances, will count as possible confirmers or disconfirmers of my claim, because given what we know about the way things go, it is only persons in such circumstances that could be expected to see a fir tree if there is one there. Similar points can be made about the other modes of testing. Since 1. is just a special case of 2., we can concentrate on the latter.

It would seem that theistic practice does not exhibit these features.

1. and 2. Religious experience does not put us in a position to make predictions about the divine, despite the persistent claims of apocalyptic groups. God, so far as we can tell from our experience, does not operate in accordance with any regularities discernible by us. We are not able to anticipate God's punishment or forgiveness, the granting or withdrawing of His grace. No more are we able to anticipate where, when, or under what conditions He will enter into a human being's experience. Hence, we are not in a position to devise checking precedures, to specify what experiences some other subject would have under certain conditions if what the first subject reported of God is correct.

3. RE is not a common possession of mankind in the way PP is. This divides into two points. (A) Many people do not engage in RE at all. This includes both those who do not take themselves to be experiencing any divine or transcendent reality at all (some of whom are religious believers), and those who objectify religious experience with schemes quite different from those of theistic religions. (B) Most of the practitioners of RE are aware of the presence of God only fleetingly and, for the most part, uncertainly. Awareness of God is usually a dim, elusive matter, lacking in detail and vividness and eminently subject to doubt. It is like seeing something in a dense fog, or, in a more traditional phrase, through a glass, darkly. All this is in sharp contrast to the clarity, detail, persistence, and irresistible convincingness of sense perception.

4. It hardly requires mention that religious experience gets objectified in terms of radically different conceptual schemes in different religious traditions. The same general sort of experience that a Christian takes to be an awareness of the presence of a supreme personal deity, might be taken in Hindu circles as an experienced identity of the self with a supreme undifferentiated unity. Where individuals experience God as communicating something to them, these messages will differ in ways that, generally but not invariably, correspond to the locally

dominant theology.

Before coming to grips with the alleged epistemic bearing of these differences, I want to make two preliminary points. (1) We have to engage in PP to determine that this practice has features 1.-4., and that CP lacks them. Apart from observation we have no way of knowing that, e.g., while all cultures agree in their way of cognizing the physical environment they differ in their ways of cognizing the divine, or that PP puts us in a position to predict while CP doesn't. It might be thought that this is loading the dice in favor of my opponent. If we are to use PP, rather than some neutral source, to determine what features it has, shouldn't the same courtesy of self-assessment be accorded CP? Why should it be judged on the basis of what we learn about it from another practice, while that other practice is allowed to grade itself? To be sure, this is a serious issue only if answers to these questions are forthcoming from CP that differ from those we arrive at by engaging in PP. Fortunately I can avoid getting involved in these issues by ruling that what I am interested in here is how CP looks from the standpoint of PP. The person I am primarily concerned to address is one who, like all the rest of us, engages in PP and supposes it to be generally reliable. My aim is to show this person that, on his own grounds, CP enjoys basically the same epistemic status as PP. Hence it is consonant with my purposes to allow PP to determine the facts of the matter with respect to both practices. (2) I could quibble over whether the contrast is as sharp as is alleged. Questions could be raised about both sides of the putative divide. On the PP side, is it really true that all cultures have objectified sense experience in the same way? Many anthropologists have thought not. And what about the idea that all normal adult human beings engage in the same perceptual practice? Aren't we loading the dice by taking participation in what we regard as standard perceptual practice as our basic criterion for normality? On the CP side, is it really the case that this practice reveals no regularities to us, or only that they are very different from regularities in the physical world? What about the point that God is faithful to His promises? Or that the pure in heart will see God? However, I believe that when all legitimate quibbles have been duly registered there will still be very significant difference between the two practices in these respects. So rather than contesting the factual allegations, I will concentrate on the de jure issue as to what bearing these differences have on epistemic status.

Why suppose that the lack of these features constitutes an adequate, or even a significant, reason for taking RE to be unreliable? I can see that 1.-4. are desiderata for an epistemic practice. If we were shaping the world to our heart's desire, we would arrange for our practices to exhibit these features. Since PP possesses them and RE does not, the former is, to that extent and in that way, superior. But, granting all that, why should we suppose that the lack of these features is incompatible with reliability?

Presumably, one who thinks this is reasoning as follows. In the case of PP these features are manifestations of reliability (13). It is because PP is reliable that it yields successful predictions, that its practitioners tend to agree, and so on. These are ways in which its reliability shows itself. Therefore, when we encounter a practice that lacks these manifestations, we can conclude that it also lacks reliability; otherwise analogous manifestations would be forthcoming.

The trouble with this is that it assumes that reliability will manifest itself in these ways wherever and whenever it is found, and without specific reasons for assuming that we are not entitled to the assumption. It is certainly not true in general that when a state or condition manifests itself by M in certain cases, it will yield M wherever it is found. Being a good philosopher sometimes, but not always, manifests itself by the production of many important writings. Anger sometimes, but not always, shows itself in increased volume of speech. And so on. Why should we suppose that the reliability of an epistemic practice always shows itself in features like 1.-4.? I can see no warrant for any such supposition. So far as I can see, it is just a kind of parochialism that makes the lack of 1.-4. seem to betoken unreliability. One uncritically takes salient features of PP, ways in which reliability shows itself there, as necessary conditions of reliability.

I will now, in conclusion, support this judgment by indicating how RE, in particular, could well be reliable in the absence of 1.-4. I shall sketch out a possible state of affairs in which RE is quite trustworthy while lacking 1.-4., and then suggest that we have no reason to suppose that this state of affairs does not obtain.

Suppose, then, that (A) God is too different from created beings, too "wholly other," for us to be able to grasp any regularities in His behavior. Suppose further that (B) for the same reasons we can only attain the faintest, sketchiest, and most insecure grasp of what God is like. Finally, suppose that (C) God has decreed that a human being will be aware of His presence in any clear and unmistakable fashion only when certain special and difficult conditions are satisfied. If all this is the case, then it is the reverse of surprising that RE should lack 1.-4. even if it does involve a genuine experience of God. It would lack 1.-2. because of (A). It is quite understandable that it should lack 4. because of (B). If our cognitive powers are not fitted to frame an adequate conception of God, it is not at all surprising that there should be wide variation in attempts to do so. This is what typically happens in science when investigators are grappling with a phenomenon no one really understands. A variety of models, analogues, metaphors, hypotheses, hunches are propounded, and it is impossible to secure universal agreement. 3. is missing because of (C). If very difficult conditions are set, it is not surprising that few are chosen. Now it is compatible with (A)-(C) that (D) religious experience should, in general, constitute a

47

genuine awareness of the divine, and that (E) although any
particular articulation of such an experience might be mistaken to
a greater or lesser extent, indeed even though all such
articulations might miss the mark to some extent, still such
judgments will for the most part contain some measure of truth;
and that (F) God's designs contain provision for correction and
refinement, for increasing the accuracy of the beliefs derived
from religious experience. If something like (A)-(F) is the case,
then RE is trustworthy even though it lacks features 1.-4. This
is a conceivable way in which RE would constitute a road to the
truth, while differing from PP in respects 1.-4. Therefore, unless
we have adequate reason for supposing that (A)-(F) does not
obtain, as we do not, we cannot infer the unreliability of RE from
the lack of 1.-4.

Moreover, it is not just that (A)-(C) constitute a bare
possibility. In the practice of RE we seem to learn that this is
the way things are. As for (A) and (B), it is the common teaching
of all the higher religions that God is of a radically different
order of being from finite substances and, therefore, that we
cannot expect to attain the grasp of His nature and His doings
that we have of worldly objects. As for (C), it is a basic theme
in Christianity, and in other religions as well, that one finds
God within one's experience, to any considerable degree, only as
one progresses in the spiritual life. God is not available for
voyeurs. Awareness of God, and understanding of His nature and
His will for us, is not a purely cognitive achievement; it
requires the involvement of the whole person; it takes a practical
commitment and a practice of the life of the spirit, as well as
the exercise of cognitive faculties.

To be sure, if in the last paragraph I were arguing for the
reliability of RE by alleging that (A)-(C) obtain, then that
argument would be vitiated with circularity since we have no
reason for supposing that (A)-(C) obtain, apart from assuming the
reliability of RE, or some other religious epistemic practice.
But that was not the point. In calling attention to the fact that
RE yields (A)-(C), I was merely reinforcing the negative point
that we lack adequate reason for supposing that these conditions
do not obtain. So far from that being the case, insofar as any
epistemic practice claims to tell us anything about the matter,
what it tells us is that they do obtain. Thus the basic point is
still the negative one. We do not have adequate reason for
supposing that (A)-(F) do not obtain, and, therefore, we are not
justified in taking the absence of 1.-4. to establish the
unreliability of RE.

VIII

I conclude that M-beliefs have basically the same epistemic status as P-beliefs, and that one who regards the latter as <u>prima facie</u> justified by experience is in no position to deny that status to the former.

NOTES

1. Being <u>based</u> on adequate reasons is one form of this, but not the only possible form. There can also be reliable ways in which a belief arises from experience.

2. It should be abundantly clear that, contrary to what might be the suggestion of the term, we are <u>not</u> taking epistemic practices to involve <u>voluntary</u> actions.

3. This indicates a crucial connection between Jn and Jr. Even though one can be Jn without being Jr, still one can be Jn only if one's belief doesn't stem from failures to attempt to make one's belief-forming practices reliable and hence to make one's beliefs Jr. Being Jn, we might say, is to have aimed as one should at being Jr.

4. The main difference between this idealized formulation and the more realistic one is that where we are unable to prevent ourselves from engaging in an epistemic practice, we will thereby be Jn in the beliefs that emerge from it, whatever its reliability and whatever we have reason to think of its reliability. Whereas on the simplifying assumption, that complexity is washed out.

5. The reader will note that our fundamental intellectual obligation, according to II., has to do only with refraining from epistemic practices; nothing is said as to conditions under which we are obliged to engage in practices. I don't want to deny that we have a purely intellectual obligation to engage in belief-forming practices, but the conditions under which one is so obliged would be very difficult to spell out. It obviously won't do to take the simplest tack and say that one is obliged to engage in a practice <u>iff</u> it is reliable. Assuming that there are several reliable practices, that would leave us with an intolerable multiplicity of jointly unfulfillable obligations. (That same point would hold on the "reasons" formulation to be presented next, provided there is a multiplicity of practices concerning which we have the appropriate reasons.) Of course, one could say that we have a <u>prima facie</u> obligation to engage in each reliable practice at any given time, but that this is often overridden by

more pressing obligations. But even this is untenable. Suppose that at this moment I have no other pressing obligations at all. It still seems false that I am obliged to engage in the practice of acquiring information about Attic vase painting from the Encyclopedia Britannica, just on the grounds that this is a reliable epistemic practice and/or one that I have adequate reason to regard as reliable. What we want in the way of a positive obligation is, roughly speaking, an obligation to engage in practices of the proper sort a reasonable proportion of the time. For the purposes of this paper I do not need to get into all that. The obligation to refrain will be sufficient to generate the problems I need to consider here.

6. There are, of course, various positions that are intermediate between these pure extremes. Thus one might hold that one is obliged to abstain from a practice if one has <u>some</u> reason to regard it as unreliable, and no reason to regard it as reliable. In this short discussion we shall have to restrict ourselves to the simplest alternatives.

7. T-practices might be called "inferential" practices, but because of persistent unclarity over the boundaries of that term I have avoided it.

8. Before considering PP and RE specifically, let's note that it is not possible to demonstrate reliability, or to provide reasons of any sort for or against, <u>all</u> our epistemic practices. For in order to provide non-circular reasons for the reliability of a practice, P, we have to use some other practice to acquire those reasons. Whatever practice we use, we are assuming <u>it</u> to be reliable in putting forward those reasons; and so if <u>it</u> were P that we were using, we would be assuming its reliability in order to establish its reliability. But if we are using some other practice, Q, then in order to provide reasons for its reliability we have to use some practice other than P or Q, if we are not to fall into circularity. It is easy to see that unless we are to generate an infinite regress or fall at some point into circularity, we must at some point simply rely on the reliability of a practice without being able to show that it is reliable. Nor does this argument presuppose a foundationalist conception of the structure of knowledge. Assume a coherence theory. Then to show that P is reliable we would show that the assumption of its reliability coheres with S (the system coherence with which is our supreme test). Now if P is <u>not</u> C, the practice of accepting beliefs on the basis of coherence with S, all is well so far. But now what about the question of the reliability of C? If that reliability is shown by alleging coherence with C, we are involved in circularity. If not, we must use another practice to garner support for C, and we are off to the races again.

9. This could be flushed out by a challenge to our procedure. If

we were asked why we supposed ourselves to know that such and such a prediction was made and borne out, if the inquiry were pushed sufficiently far, and if we were sufficiently reflective and candid, we would eventually be forced to claim the reliability of PP in supporting our procedure.

10. In a recent article James van Cleve (1979) has sought to absolve Descartes from the famous charge of circularity. He points out that when Descartes uses clear and distinct perceptions to obtain the premises he then uses to prove the existence of God, from which he derives the conclusion that clear and distinct perceptions are reliable, he is not guilty of logical circularity, since the claim of the reliability of clear and distinct perception does not itself appear among the premises. Van Cleve does not seem to find the epistemic circularity involved to be disturbing. And, indeed, something is to be said for this position. As van Cleve points out, if it is merely true that all clear and distinct perceptions are true, then Descartes will be justified in accepting propositions beacause he clearly and distinctly perceives them, even if he does not know, and is not justified in believing, the proposition that all clear and distinct perceptions are true. Thus Descartes could become justified by this procedure in accepting the general principle, provided it was true all along; he wouldn't have had to be justified antecedently in believing it.

11. These arguments have not generally been explicitly cast as arguments for the reliability of PP, but something like that is part of what the argument seeks to establish.

12. Unfortunately, the argument of this paper depends on three assumptions I have not been able to support. (1) There are no adequate reasons for the reliability of PP. (2) There are no adequate reasons for the reliability of RE. (3) We cannot use philosophical reasoning to establish conclusions that generally disconfirm the deliverances of RE.

13. This point must not be put by saying: "These features give us an adequate reason for taking PP to be reliable." Since we can only ascertain these features by using PP, any such reasoning would be infected with epistemic circularity.

The Epistemology of William James and Early Buddhism

David J. Kalupahana

William James was an empiricist. So was Siddhartha Gautama who became a Buddha. They certainly were not rationalists. Therefore, in our examination of their epistemology, it would not be necessary for us to make comparisons with rationalism or even with a rationalist conception of truth as coherence. Although they were empiricists, they were empiricists of a completely different order. This is what I propose to highlight in the course of this paper. For this reason, it becomes necessary for me to draw your attention to what is generally known as "empiricism" in Western philosophy, make a few general remarks about it and then proceed to examine the epistemological standpoints of James as well as Buddha.

I could start with the well-known empiricist of the Western world: Aristotle, who is believed to have broken ranks with his teacher, Plato, because the latter was a rationalist of the highest order. John Dewey's analysis of Aristotle's philosophy is revealing (1). According to him, Aristotle, the empiricist, was not different from Plato, the rationalist, especially when we come to consider the former's First Philosophy. The reason why we consider Plato and Aristotle to be poles apart is the false or the apparent distinction made during that time between religion and philosophy. The change from religion to philosophy appeared so great in _form_ that their identity as to _content_ was simply ignored or forgotten. For Aristotle, the difference between religion and philosophy pertain merely to language and not to content. He thought that from remote antiquity tradition had handed down the idea that heavenly bodies are gods, but this idea was expressed in story form. This discursive language, embroidered with myth and legend, concealed the core of truth about heavenly bodies.

Therefore, the negative work of philosophy was to strip away these imaginative accretions. This was why the ordinary man considered philosophy to be a destructive discipline. But there was another aspect of this philosophic enterprise which the masses did not understand. That was the positive contribution of philosophy. The belief that the divine encompasses the world was detached from its mythical context and made the basis of philosophy, and it became also the foundation of physical science. Avoidance of myth and legend, emotion and imagination, and presenting the story of the universe in a rational discourse gave rise to one of the greatest tools of the Anglo-European philosophical traditions, namely, logic as a rational science. Aristotle's own First Philosophy, or what we call metaphysics, had to conform to this logic. Such conformity conferred upon the

53

objects of First Philosophy necessary and immutable characteristics. Communion with this unchangeable truth is what every philosopher since Aristotle aspired to.

The empiricists of the modern world are no more different in their endeavors. They too were looking for indubitable truths. The only difference pertained to the method they adopted in arriving at such indubitable truths. We all are familiar with the claims of the empiricists that the answer to skepticism is to be found in the deliverances of sense, not of reason. One of their basic assumptions is that we can build up or construct genuine knowledge from certain basic elements about which we have no doubts, that is, those that are clear and distinct. Locke's "ideas of sense," Berkeley's "ideas" or "sensible qualities," Hume's "impressions," Russell's "sense data" - all these can be understood as the empiricist attempt to express the indubitable truth about the world. Russell went so far as to construct an ideal language in which these indubitable truths could be expressed, and this language, it may be mentioned, was not free from the two-valued logic that dominated Aristotle's First Philosophy. Indeed, one of Russell's favorite philosophical treatises - Wittgenstein's Tractatus - tried to state in no unclear terms what the ultimate truth about the world is. One of the victims of that theory was the human will, which came to be banished from the world to a transcendent sphere. It was not a far cry from that of Immanuel Kant who, though inspired by an empiricist like Hume, ended up being a transcendentalist looking for laws that guide the starry sky above and the moral life below.

I made these few very general comments on the Anglo-European philosophical tradition in order to highlight one basic characteristic common to its apparently divergent theories of truth. The two theories of truth are the rationalist theory of coherence and the empiricist theory of correspondence. Their common characteristic is "essentialism." This essentialism is the foundation of the Anglo-European theories of knowledge, theories of truth and theories of morality, nay, even anything that can be called a "theory."

If there is any originality in American philosophy, anything that can distinguish it from other Western philosophical traditions, it is opposition to this essentialism. Anti-essentialism is the hallmark of the radical empiricism and pragmatism propounded by one of the greatest American philosophers: the Harvard philosopher and psychologist, William James. Unfortunately, the dominant influence of the essentialist tradition, better known by the characterization Santayana gave to it as the "genteel tradition" (2), has kept this great philosopher out of the limelight. This dominance of essentialism has earned for Charles Sanders Peirce the praise of the philosophical community here as the greatest of pragmatists, so much so that even a philosophical society has been founded in his honor. No such respect is shown for William James, who is rejected by the essentialist philosophers as a mere psychologist, and by the

54

behaviorist psychologists as a mere philosopher. One philosopher who was able to overcome these prejudices recently remarked:

> One symptom of this incorrect focus is a tendency to overpraise Peirce. Peirce is praised partly because he developed various logical notions and various technical problems (such as the counterfactual conditional) which were taken up by the logical empiricists....His contribution to pragmatism was merely to have given its name, and to have stimulated James. Peirce himself remained the most Kantian of thinkers - the most convinced that philosophy gave us an all-embracing ahistorical context in which every other species of discourse could be assigned its proper place and rank. It was just this Kantian assumption that there was such a context, and that epistemology or semantics could discover it, against which James and Dewey reacted. We need to focus on this reaction if we are to recapture a proper sense of their importance (3).

Peirce's pragmatism is rooted in the Anglo-European philosophical tradition and does not possess the same kind of originality that can be found in James's or Dewey's, who were responsible for breaking away completely from the fundamentally essentialist standpoint of that philosophical tradition. I shall confine myself to the philosophy of William James, who is really responsible for setting the tone of the new anti-essentialist pragmatism in America.

James's first philosophical essay was "The Sentiment of Rationality" and was written in 1880, the year he was appointed assistant professor of philosophy at Harvard. Although it is an essay that every student of philosophy in this country must have read, it is difficult to come across one who has heard of it. This essay not only repudiated the essentialist standpoint of the yet unwritten Old Testament of modern Western philosophy - Wittgenstein's Tractatus - but also heralded the ideas embodied in the New Testament, i.e., Wittgenstein's Philosophical Investigations. The concluding paragraph of this lengthy essay reads:

> The ultimate philosophy, we may therefore conclude, must not be too straight-laced in form, must not in all its parts divide heresy from orthodoxy by too sharp a line (4).

This would indeed weaken the system of two-valued logic which has created all the dilemmas in the Western philosophical tradition since Plato. The problems that we run into when trying to understand James's thought are enormous. The foremost among them is the fact that he had no theories. When we consider his statement regarding ultimate philosophy, quoted above, he could not have theories. This is an aspect of his anti-essentialism that came to be noted only recently:

> As long as we see James or Dewey as having "theories of truth" or "theories of knowledge" or "theories of morality," we shall get them wrong. We shall ignore their criticisms of the assumption that there ought to be theories about such matters. We shall not see how radical their thought was - how deep was their criticism of the attempt, common to Kant, Husserl, Russell and C. I. Lewis, to make philosophy into a foundational discipline (5).

Since James did not have theories and since he was sufficiently open-minded to accept and anticipate various possibilities in his open-ended conception of the universe, those of us looking for clear-cut theories regarding this and that are going to be very disappointed. This, indeed, is the most formidable psychological problem we are going to be confronted with in reading James. But if we do not have any such expectations, reading James's thought could turn out to be one of the most exhilarating experiences one can have.

Time would not permit me to deal with each and every idea expressed by James. I shall therefore confine myself to a few notions which I think are important and then go on to compare them with those of an Asian tradition that preceded James by almost 2500 years.

Although James's name is generally associated with pragmatism, his major contribution to Western philosophy lies in his formulation of radical empiricism. His challenge against essentialism is contained in his radical empiricism, rather than in pragmatism, and, indeed a careful analysis of these two notions would reveal that pragmatism gains respectability and can be saved from misinterpretations if it is studied in relation to radical empiricism.

The essentialists, starting from Plato, were looking for "things as they are." Kant is believed to have made the most startling assertion when he claimed that we cannot know "things as they are" through sense perception. It is the implication of the "Copernican Revolution" in philosophy that Kant claimed he brought about and with which he is credited. It is the view that if space and time are contributed by the knowing mind, spatial and temporal objects will be altered in the very act of being apprehended. Reason too, according to him, lacks the intuitive powers and

56

therefore we cannot be acquainted with "things as they are" through that means. Yet, the essentialism embedded in Kant's bloodstream surfaced again when he claimed that reason possesses concepts of its own, concepts such as possibility, existence, necessity, substance and cause, through which it can arrive at what may be called "symbolic cognition" of such things. In other words, reason can reveal some true propositions about them. For example, a concept such as a "perfect being" which is the reality (as opposed to appearance) underlying everything and in terms of which other things can be measured and evaluated, can be formed by the intellect in its real, as opposed to logical, use (6). James would not have anything to do with such speculation. For him, "things as they really are" are unknowable, period.

What kind of knowledge can man reasonably claim? If "things as they are" are unknowable, what are the things that are revealed to us in experience? According to my understanding of James's epistemology, man can at best claim to know "things as they have come to be," i.e., in the context in which they have arisen. This seems to be the most important idea behind radical empiricism, an idea which has escaped the attention of many a critic of James.

Let us begin with James's explanation of experience. It is embodied in his famous dictum, often misquoted and misunderstood by leading interpreters of James, that experience is a "big blooming buzzing confusion" (7).

This brief statement occurs in his last major philosophical work published posthumously, viz., Some Problems of Philosophy (1911). Yet it represents not only a summary of the 1377 pages of his monumental work, The Principles of Psychology (1890), but also a summation of his entire philosophical career covering more than thirty years. Scholars who made piecemeal studies of James's radical empiricism and pragmatism have tended to completely ignore this extremely succinct explanation of experience. A careful examination of this four-word definition would provide clarification for many a problem that interpreters as well as opponents of James have raised.

According to this definition, our experience is big in that when we have experience we are bombarded by a huge mass of sensory stimuli. James referred to this mass of sensory stimuli as the "aboriginal sensible muchness" (8). This "aboriginal sensible muchness" is not to be confused with a mosaic mass of discrete "impressions" or "sense data" coming to us without any relations or connections. What the cognitive mind does is not to provide relations or connections between discrete impressions, as Hume believed, or to provide form, as Kant maintained, but to select out of this "aboriginal sensible muchness" of related impressions those in which the perceiving mind has an interest, for it could not deal with this entire mass. It is for this reason that this experience also becomes a source of confusion. It is unavoidable that in this process of selection, some elements are left out and others registered with greater intensity. While the "aboriginal sensible muchness" is not known because of the limitations of the

57

human mind, what the mind picks up from that "aboriginal sensible muchness" is what eventually comes to be designated as truth. Therefore, Joseph Runzo is correct when he rejected the views of those essentialist interpreters of James who made a clear-cut distincion between a "cognitive" truth and "pragmatic" truth (9). In other words, radical empiricism and pragmatism are not two distinct conceptions but are very closely interwoven; they cannot even be studied separately.

Next, experience turns out to be a blooming affair, with a gradually opening horizon, each segment of experience contributing its share to the subsequent. Here again, depending upon the interest of the cognitive mind, certain elements are dropped and some others picked up. Each time we pick up a new vein, we claim it to be a discovery. Truth is thus not ready-made, but made by the cognitive mind.

Finally, such an experience cannot be a lifeless one, as it would turn out to be in a world of perfect correspondence. It is buzzing with life, with new life. As a reptile casts out its old skin with the growth of a fresh one, so is freshness instilled into experience. It is never static, but continues to change into something else.

James was able to present this explanation of experience because he rejected the age-old rationalistic conception of time and adopted a more empirical notion suggested by E. R. Clay. He quotes Clay's words as follows:

> The relation of experience to time has not been profoundly studied. Its objects are given as being of the present, but the part of time referred to by the datum is a very different thing from the conterminous of the past and the future which philosophy denotes by the name Present. The present to which the datum refers is really a part of the past - a recent past - delusively given as being a time that intervenes between the past and the future. Let it be named the specious present, and let the past, that is given as being the past, be known as the obvious past. All the notes of a bar of a song seems to the listener to be contained in the present. All the changes of place of a meteor seems to the beholder to be contained in the present. At the instant of the termination of such series, no part of the time measured by them seems to be a past. Time, then, considered relatively to human apprehension, consists of four parts, viz., the obvious past, the specious present, the real present and the future. Omitting the specious present, it consists of three...nonentities - the past which does not

exist, the future which does not exist and
their conterminous, the present; the faculty
from which it proceeds lies to us in the
fiction of the specious present (10).

On the basis of this, James concludes that practically
cognized present is no knife-edge, but a saddleback, with a
certain breadth of its own on which we sit perched, and from which
we look into two directions into time. The unit of composition of
our perception of time is a duration, with a bow and a stern, as
it were - a rearward - and a foreward-looking end (11).

Armed with this notion of time and conception of experience,
James went on to speak about empiricism, but qualified it in order
to distinguish it from the more popular British empiricism. This
qualification is what brought about the "Jamesean Revolution" in
Western philosophy and is clearly embodied in James's criticism of
Hume. Putting it very graphically, James maintained that Humean
empiricism takes into account only the perchings of a bird,
whereas radical empiricism recognizes the flights as well (12).
For him, the flights are as important as anything else in
understanding the perchings. Similarly, things cannot be
separated from their surroundings except for a conceptual
analysis, which analysis is a mere substitution. Therefore, he
concludes,

> The intellectual life of man consists almost
> wholly in his substitution of a conceptual
> order for the perceptual order in which his
> experience originally comes (13).

James believed that this substituted order is static (14).
Therefore, it cannot maintain a relationship of perfect
correspondence to the cognitive-pragmatic order all the time, for
the latter, as explained above, is continually blooming and
buzzing with new life, with new information. It is for this
reason that the conceptual order has to be constantly checked and
re-checked in the light of the cognitive-pragmatic order.
Therefore, when someone calls for a definition of truth, James
would respond by saying that truth is what "works" (15).
Philosophical propositions are part and parcel of the conceptual
order, and truth and falsity, therefore, pertain to that order.
Attempts to determine truth or falsity of philosophical
propositions taken in "themselves" have led to all kinds of
theories of meaning, of semantics. James was not ready to involve
himself in such an essentialist enterprise. Pragmatism for him was
not another theory of meaning holding its own sovereignty. Being
a mere substitution, it depended on the perceptual order and we
need to guard ourselves against considering that conceptual order
to be absolute. Therefore, the method by which we discover the
meaning of philosophical propositions is by the examination of
their particular practical consequences in experience. Thus,

pragmatism is not a theory of truth attempting to clarify the idea
of meaning; rather, it is an attempt to clarify the meaning of
"ideas" we form on the basis of experience.

Critics of pragmatism find the concept of "cash-value" to be
obnoxious, offensive and objectionable. Russell, the apostle of
the essentialist tradition during the modern period, decries it,
saying:

> Scepticism is the very essence of pragmatic
> philosophy: nothing is certain, everything is
> liable to revision, and the attainment of any
> truth in which we can rest securely is
> impossible. It is, therefore, not worthwhile
> to trouble our heads about what is true; ...
> (16).

The most appropriate answer to this criticism may be found in
The Quest for Certainty (1929) by John Dewey, who was James's
faithful companion in the anti-essentialist movement. The refusal
to recognize certainty with regard to empirical knowledge need not
lead to skepticism. Thus, the acceptance of pragmatism as a
criterion for deciding what is true and false does not necessarily
mean that one has to accept wayward fancies, utopias and delusions
as constituting truth. Pragmatism would lend itself to such
corruption only if it is divorced from radical empiricism.
Unfortunately for Russell and other critics of pragmatism, radical
empiricism was almost nonexistent as a concept when they made
their criticisms. They failed to realize that although the term
was coined by James after they wrote his Pragmatism, yet the
unnamed radical empiricism, which was so clearly expounded in The
Principles of Psychology, was the very basis of that pragmatism.

In The Principles of Psychology, James distinguished between
"knowledge of acquaintance" and "knowledge about" (17). His
notion of acquaintance is what we have discussed so far.
Referring to "knowledge about," he says:

> All the elementary natures of the world, its
> highest genera, the simple qualities of matter
> and mind, together with the kinds of relation
> that subsist between them, must either not be
> known at all, or known in this dumb way of
> acquaintance without knowledge about. In
> minds able to speak at all there is, it is
> true, some knowledge about everything. Things
> can at least be classed, and the times of
> their appearance told (18).

It is true that if one were to depend entirely upon this
knowledge about, one could end outside the real world altogether,
in wayward fancies, utopias, fictions or mistakes. But James does
not emphasize complete dependence upon this knowledge. Instead,

he insisted upon adopting the empiricist method of verification in the light of knowledge of acquaintance. Thus we adopt hypotheses on the basis of knowledge about and continue to check and re-check their truth value in the light of knowledge of acquaintance which, as pointed out earlier, is itself not absolute. So long as they produce results, we accept them as being true. When they do not work for us, we modify them or abandon them. We need such hypotheses, not only in our scientific experiments, but also in our experimentations with spiritual or religious phenomena.

The adoption of the experimental method, not only in the matter of verifying the truth or falsity relating to our physical environment but also with regard to religious or spiritual phenomena, distinguished James from many other main-line philosophers of his day. He seems to have realized that the difficulties we encounter in dealing with religious or spiritual phenomena are similar to, or even greater than, the problems we face in dealing with our physical environment. These difficulties did not compel James to leave out such phenomena, saying: "Whereof one cannot speak, thereof one must be silent." He wanted to find out whether such phenomena are part and parcel of our "aboriginal sensible muchness." Therefore, without throwing them into a completely different sphere, a sphere to be considered transcendent, James decided to utilize the very same methods he adopted in deciding what is true or false in our physical environment. Giving up the reductionism treasured by the essentialists and adopting a radical empiricist approach as well as a pragmatic criterion of truth in the area of religious phenomena, he was able to pursue a path different from those of his colleagues even in the philosophy of religion. This enabled him, even at that early stage, to examine the truth value of God-centered religious lives as well as the God-denying spiritual traditions. The result was the epoch-making work The Varieties of Religious Experience. Theories of all sorts were given up. Respect was shown to many a religious experience, even if these did not fit in with the preconceived theories.

How his radical empiricism and pragmatism led him to an anti-essentialist standpoint in dealing with religious phenomena is clearly exemplified by the manner in which he responded to the concept of the Absolute. If someone considered the Absolute to be the foundation of the world as well as human existence, all that has been, that are and that will be, James considered it a metaphysical monster. He even startled one of his audiences when he said: "Damn the Absolute. Let the Absolute bury the Absolute" (19). It was the same kind of criticism that he would direct against a scientist who would consider a hypothesis to be the truth, who would consider knowledge about to be identical with knowledge of acquaintance. But if the Absolute were to be conceived of as a possible goal to be achieved in the future, and in that way serves some useful function in society, James had no objection to it. He felt that there is no justification in denying the truth-value of such a conception until the last man in

61

the universe had his say.

The Varieties of Religious Experience, as well as his essays and lectures published posthumously as William James on Psychical Research (1960), clearly indicate his willingness to recognize the validity of religious or spiritual phenomena which have been carefully verified and documented, even if these did not fit into any definite framework or law. Dogmatic rejection of pragmatically significant events, while courting the unseen beauty queen from the world of absolute certainty, was not what James could accommodate in his epistemology.

Such religious truths would hardly make their appearance in the laboratory of the physical scientist who prides himself being non-moral and is therefore not concerned with the moral life of man. These truths made their appearance mostly where man's moral life was the focus of concern. But when that focusing was carried out far beyond the confines of radical empiricism and pragmatism, it led to spiritual dogmatism and religious imperialism, thereby giving rise to the opposition between science and religion.

Such dogmatism and imperialism has no place in James's humanism. He realized that moral behavior varies from society to society, from individual to individual. It is even more variable than the climatic conditions surrounding man. Therefore, instead of looking for absolute moral laws or values, James adopted the pragmatic criterion for deciding what is satisfactory and unsatisfactory. He was for utilitarianism, but his utilitarianism was more humanistic. Sacrificing of the minority or even one man for the sake of the happiness of the majority was not his way of deciding what is good and bad, what is moral and immoral. The Athenian society in which Socrates lived and Socrates himself were essentialist. Hence they could not avoid a conflict. Athenian society may have survived longer and Socrates would have avoided drinking the hemlock, if only both were guided by radical empiricism and pragmatism. A careful study of these two doctrines would reveal the manner in which many a dilemma in social, political and moral life can be satisfactorily solved. Knowledge of the mysteries surrounding the world are important only to the extent that such knowledge can make man happy during his brief stay here in this world. James's radical empiricism and pragmatism, therefore, inevitably led to his humanistic ethics. His last published essay before his death in 1910, "The Moral Equivalent of War," sums up his attitude towards human knowledge and its relevance.

The above discussion of the Western philosophical tradition reiterated the fact that the essentialist tradition dominated Western philosophy for nearly 2500 years until the time of William James. But in India, a similar essentialist tradition preceded Buddha by another 2500 years. It culminated in one of the most absolutist systems the world ever saw. It is the doctrine of Atman/Brahman in the Upanisads, which subsequently was presented in the most dogmatic form in the locus classicus of the Hindu religion - the Bhagavadgita.

WILLIAM JAMES AND EARLY BUDDHISM

In his famous discourse to the Kalamas (20), a group of people living in a little-known township called Kesaputta, Buddha set out the tone of his epistemology. The Kalamas complained to Buddha that different teachers approached them and each presented a theory that ran counter to what others presented as the truth about the world. Buddha's first and foremost advice to them was that in such a situation they should suspend judgment, without merely following tradition, report or hearsay, without being misled by scriptures, without undue reliance on logic and a priori reasoning, without depending on mere form or on reflection and approval of some theory, or the mere appropriateness of a theory or even through respect for a teacher. Having suspended judgment, they were to adopt a radical empiricist approach in order to discover, not how things are, but how things have come to be (yathabhuta) (21).

The primary source of this knowledge, according to Buddha, is sense experience (sanna). Sense experience is explained in the early discourses thus:

> Depending upon the visual organ and the visible object arises visual consciousness. The harmonious combination of these three is contact; depending upon contact arises feeling or sensation. What one feels or senses, one perceives; what one perceives, one reflects about; what one reflects about, one is obsessed with. What one is obsessed with, due to that, concepts characterized by obsessed perceptions assail him in regard to visible objects cognizable by the visual organ, belonging to the past, future and present (This statement is repeated with regard to other sense faculties.)(22)

A student of William James cannot help being fascinated by this very terse statement, in that it embodies not only radical empiricism and pragmatism, but also James's views about the perceptual and conceptual orders. Here feeling or sensation is the most important element of human experience. It is dependent on the sense organ, the object of sense and self-consciousness arising on occasion of sense perception. Feeling cannot be studied without reference to these three factors, for any variation in these factors would be reflected in the sort of feeling one has. This radical empiricist explanation is then immediately changed. Instead of saying: "Depending upon feeling, arises perception," the text goes on to say: "What one feels, one perceives," thereby changing the whole grammatical structure of the sentence, the formula now taking a personal approach suggestive of deliberate activity. Here then is pragmatism built into radical empiricism. The implication is that since the sensation is a big blooming buzzing confusion, selective attention

63

carves its objects of preference out of the "aboriginal sensible muchness," such selective activity being prompted by the difficulties involved in dealing with that "sensible muchness." This carving out is done according to one's likes and dislikes and, therefore, it has been pointed out that, at this point, Buddha anticipated the emergence of the ego-consciousness (23). This is the so-called perceptual order, not a purely objective one but one in which objectivity is inextricably mixed up with one's subjectivity. From this relatively objective order, a person proceeds to form his concepts with which he then gets obsessed, which he holds onto without having the courage to give up, sometimes against overwhelming perceptual evidence. It is such conceptual obsession that prevented people from accepting even the discoveries of men like Galileo and Copernicus. For Buddha, such conceptual obsessions constitute the root of most human conflict and suffering. It produces dogmatism of the highest order.

One way to overcome this dogmatism, according to Buddha, is by setting up mindfulness (satipatthana) (24). It is this setting up of mindfulness that enabled Buddha to become the foremost anti-essentialist in the world. The doctrine of non-substantiality (anatta, anatman), emphasizing the absence of a permanent and immutable self or substance in man as well as in the world, was the direct result of this setting up of mindfulness. Buddha called it "a veritable path leading to the realization of truth and the consequent overcoming of suffering and unhappiness and the attainment of peace and happiness" (25).

The setting up of mindfulness represents Buddha's greatest contribution to the contemplative or meditative tradition in India. The pre-Buddhist contemplatives believed that by retiring into the forest and sitting cross-legged and concentrating one's mind, one is able to perceive directly the Atman or Brahman which they considered to be the one ultimate reality or essence in man and the universe (26). Buddha, who practiced meditation for six years following the instructions given by some of the contemplatives of India, like Alara Kalama and Uddaka Ramaputta, failed to perceive such an ultimate reality or essence (27). Yet he did not abandon meditation as some of the Materialists did. Instead, he let meditation lead him to whatever information it could lead. This is setting up of mindfulness.

He set up mindfulness in relation to four items, namely, his body (kaya), his sensations (vedana), his thoughts (citta) and, finally, phenomena in general (dhamma). These four items would seem to exhaust all areas of relevant human knowledge. Buddha, following his experience, advised his disciples to perceive reflectively body, sensations, thoughts and phenomena. The most important term here is anupassi, and sometimes the term anupassana occurs in this connection. The verb passati (derived from the same Indo-European root from which we get the verb 'spy') means 'to see' or 'to perceive.' With the prefix anu (which literally means 'following'), anupassati would mean "to perceive reflectively." Hence, anupassi, "one who perceives reflectively," and anupassana, "perceiving reflectively."

Such reflective perception was necessitated by the failure of the other method Buddha used, namely, "perceiving things as they truly are." But if we still desire to pour new wine into old bottles, we may maintain that "perceiving things as they truly are" is to be achieved, not by looking for essences, but by seeing how things have come to be (yathabhuta). This could not be very different from the Jamesean explanation, quoted above, that "the practically cognized present is no knife-edge, but a saddleback, with a certain breadth of its own on which we sit perched and from which we look into two directions into time." It is the radical empiricist's way of perceiving.

Adopting this method of perceiving, what did Buddha learn about his body, his sensations, his thoughts and phenomena in general? It is not possible to repeat the entire discourse here. Summarizing the discourse, it may be said that such a method revealed how the body functioned, how sensations come to be conditioned, how thoughts are formed and how phenomena in the world come to be constituted. Each explanation ends with the following statement: "Perceiving or reflecting: 'There is the body,' his mindfulness is established precisely to the extent necessary just for knowledge, just for remembrance and he fares along independently of and not grasping anything in the world" (28). This statement is repeated with regard to other items.

This last statement is crucial for any understanding of Buddha's epistemological standpoint. This perception is adopted only in so far as it yields "mere knowledge" (nanamattaya), not for the sake of formulating closed systems or theories (ditthi). The door is left open for new information that may come in the future. Hence his attitude of not grasping onto that knowledge as the only valid knowledge. It is not surprising therefore to see Buddha very often making the remark: "It is only a stupid person who would insist: 'This alone is true, everything else is false' (29), a statement so strikingly similar to that James made in concluding his essay on "The Sentiment of Rationality" quoted above.

Meditation thereby became not a voluntary exile from life, as it was for the recluses, yogins and forest dwellers of pre-Buddhist India, but a way of understanding the daily affairs of human life. It was not divorced from the work-a-day life of a human being; instead it became part and parcel of his life. This was the greatest contribution of Buddha to the contemplative life of the Indians. As one Buddhist monk, steeped in meditation, remarked:

> True meditation and mysticism do not co-exist. They are two different things. While mysticism takes us away from reality, true meditation brings us face to face with reality; for through real meditation we can see our own illusions and hallucinations face to face

> without pretence. This brings about a total transformation in our personality (30).

This experiential knowledge, when coupled with extreme and deep concentration (samahite citte), yielded a higher form of knowledge (abhinna) which include telepathy, clairvoyance and retrocognition (31). These higher forms were not different from ordinary sense knowledge in that they too were confined to what may be called the specious present; the specious present not being arbitrarily confined to the period from the emergence of self-consciousness in a person up to his death. It covered a longer time span than the sense experience of a person with unconcentrated mind. Yet, they certainly did not yield information either regarding the obvious past or the future. But the information yielded by them, especially by clairvoyance (which was defined as the knowledge of the survival of other beings) and retrocognition or knowledge of one's own past lives, were considered extremely important for an understanding of how human beings have come to be.

The early Buddhist texts emphasize the fact that these higher forms of knowledge can be developed only if a person remains "aloof from pleasures of sense and unwholesome states of mind" (vivicc' eva kamehi vivicc' eva akusalehi dhammehi) (32). This means that such perceptions are the results of a very high moral perspective. It is for this reason that Buddha maintained that moral life is a stepping stone for the attainment of higher levels of knowledge (33). It was mentioned earlier that religious truths would hardly make their appearance in the laboratory of the scientists who are not concerned with the moral life of man. Thus, for positivist philosophers who hold that ethics is beyond the scope of legitimate philosophical inquiry, such knowledge claims are illegitimate; they belong to the sphere of the transcendent or the unspeakable. The result is that the door is closed for any information that may be obtained regarding these matters even from sources other than these higher knowledges. Such sources consist of hypnotism, carefully performed by competent persons, as well as sporadic memories of adults and children regarding their past lives, which are carefully verified and documented. The work of such medical men as Dr. Ian Stevenson may be quoted as examples (34). Philosophers like James, and even C. D. Broad (35), therefore, kept the door open for such information, without rejecting them as hallucinations.

In early Buddhism, this experiential knowledge is known as knowledge of phenomena (dhamme nana) (36), and in several ways, is comparable to James's knowledge of acquaintance. It is knowledge of the specious present. Based upon that knowledge Buddha made inferences into the obvious past and the yet unknown future. Such knowledge came to be called inferential knowledge or anvaye nana (37), and it resembles, to some extent, James's knowledge about.

On the basis of knowledge of acquaintance, Buddha claimed that all phenomena experienced so far have come to be "dependently arisen" (paticcasamuppanna) (38). Extending this knowledge to the obvious past and the future, he arrived at the conception of a uniformity (dhammata) (39), explaining the "elementary natures of the world, its highest genera" which constituted the object of James's knowledge about. Buddha called it paticcasamuppada or "dependent arising" (40).

In this world of "dependent arising," Buddha perceived the nature and functioning of the human disposition (sankhara) or the human will. This phenomenal will, for Buddha, was not outside the world, but an integral part of the world of dependent arising. As James did, Buddha recognized, through experience, the undeniable validity and causal efficacy of the human will, at least on some occasions. For both Buddha and James, the fact that the human will or disposition is seen to fail sometimes did not mean that it is ineffective always. The recognition of the causal efficacy of the human will or human disposition enabled Buddha to speak of a "dispositionally conditioned world" (sankhata) within the world that is "dependently arisen" (paticcasamuppanna) (41), a world which is not much different from Karl Popper's World Three (42). Thus, he came to formulate the four truths: (1) that the world that is dispositionally conditioned is ultimately unsatisfactory, (2) that this unsatisfactoriness has a cause to account for it and that cause is attachment, (3) that that cause can be gotten rid of, which is the state of freedom from bondage or nirvana, and finally, (4) that there is a way to attain that freedom, which is the eightfold path (43).

The knowledge of "dependent arising" and the knowledge of "dispositional conditioning" provided Buddha with information of tremendous significance, for he was seeking to unravel the mysteries, not about the universe, but about man. His problem was about how man comes to experience suffering and unhappiness. Going in search of a solution to the problem of human suffering, he came up with the information regarding how man comes to be and what happens to him at death. Through retrocognition he saw for himself how his own life had been conditioned for a long long period, and how his actions contributed, along with many other factors, to his continued suffering in the world. What he saw about his own life was confirmed by his knowledge of the decrease and survival of other human beings. These carried much more certainty for him than knowledge regarding the universe. It was self-knowledge. Having gained this self-knowledge, he made a tremendous struggle to eliminate the causes that led to suffering, which he understood as excessive craving (raga, tanha) (44). Abandoning craving, and along with that hate or aversion (dosa), he was able to bring about a complete change in his psycho-physical personality as well as a complete transformation of his moral life. He attained perfect happiness. When he abandoned craving or excessive attachment, he also realized that he had eliminated craving for continued becoming in the future and that eliminated any possibility of his being reborn. He could not help but utter a paean of joy:

Destroyed is (future) birth; brought to a close is the higher life; done is what was to be done; there is no more of being such and such (45).

He claimed, with absolute certainty:

Unshakable is freedom for me; this is the last birth; there is not now any future births (for me) (46).

James began his essay on "The Sentiment of Rationality" by asking the question as to why philosophers philosophize at all. His answer was that they desire to attain a rational conception of things than the fragmentary and chaotic one which they carry with them. He then went on to ask the further question as to how a philosopher recognizes that he has attained a rational conception. This rationality is known, according to James, by certain subjective marks with which he is affected. What are these marks? The transition from the state of puzzlement and perplexity to a state of rational conception, he thought, is full of lively relief and pleasure. It produces a strong feeling of ease, peace and rest (47). It was probably this kind of lively relief and pleasure, this feeling of ease, peace and rest, that prompted Buddha and his disciples to claim with absolute certainty whatever they have achieved. Was it also this kind of feeling that prompted Wittgenstein to express the paean of joy upon the completion of his Tractatus:

On the other hand, the truth of the thoughts that are here communicated seems to me unassailable and definitive. I therefore believe myself to have found, on all essential points, the final solution of the problems (48).

Why did Wittgenstein, having made such a strong claim about the rationality he had reached, abandon that work in no time? Why did doubts start assailing him before long? Was it because Wittgenstein was, when he wrote the Tractatus, chasing the "squirrel" mentioned in James's Pragmatism?

Neither Buddha nor his disciples who attained freedom and who made similar claims ever abandoned their rationality or the sense of peace and happiness they attained as a result of that rationality. The reason seems to be that their rationality pertained to their own being, to their own personality. They had completely overcome doubt, not about the mysteries of the universe, but about themselves. This, according to Buddha, is the only kind of absolute knowledge one can attain. That knowledge was achieved as a result of a psycho-physical transformation brought about by the elimination of the burning fires within, namely, greed (lobha), hate (dosa) and confusion (moha) (49). This was the highest knowledge (panna, prajna) recognized by Buddha (50). It is popularly known as the knowledge of the cessation of defilements (asavakkhaya) (51). Although James's theory of knowledge seems to resemble that of Buddha in many respects, I am not sure whether he attained the same kind of psycho-physical and moral transformation that would have enabled him to claim this last kind of knowledge that Buddha and his disciples claimed with absolute certainty.

The "Discourse to Prince Abhaya" (Abhayarajakumara-sutta)(52) is an excellent example of Buddha's pragmatic approach relating to philosophical discourse. Confronted with a double-edged question posed by Prince Abhaya, Buddha here spoke of statements that are true or false, useful or useless, pleasant or unpleasant. These should leave us with eight types of statements as follows:

1. True   useful   pleasant

2. True   useful   unpleasant

3. True   useless   pleasant

4. True   useless   unpleasant

5. False   useful   pleasant

6. False   useful   unpleasant

7. False   useless   pleasant

8. False   useless   unpleasant

Buddha maintained that he would make statements 1 and 2, that is, those that are true and useful, whether they be pleasant or unpleasant. Yet, his non-absolutist approach induced him to make the qualification that he would make such statements depending upon the proper time (kalannu), not unconditionally. He refused to make statements that are true and useless (3, 4) and also those that are false and useless (7, 8). His pragmatism is highlighted by his refusal to make statements that are true, yet useless (3, 4). It is interesting to note that the above discourse makes no reference at all to alternatives 5 and 6, namely, those that are false and useful, whether pleasant or unpleasant. The implication seems to be that he did not recognize these as alternatives. In other words, he did not want to accept the view that a false statement could be useful. This would certainly contradict the teachings of later Mahayana according to which all linguistic statements are false but useful as means (upaya) (53). Moreover, the non-recognition of such statements would imply that, according to Buddha, wayward fancies, utopias and delusions, which are verified to be false, can have no pragmatic value at all. This is also a point which James tried ceaselessly to defend against the criticisms of the essentialist philosophers.

This leaves us with some other category of statements, namely, those that are neither true nor false. For both Buddha and James, these pertain to metaphysical issues which cannot be either proved or disproved on the basis of experience. It is with regard to such issues that both James and Buddha would say: "Whereof one cannot speak, thereof one must be silent," except, of course, when such concepts make a difference in the practical results. Buddha's attitude towards gods (54) and James's attitude towards God (55) are clear indications of their pragmatism.

NOTES

1. John Dewey, The Quest for Certainty (New York: G. P. Putnam's Sons, Capricorn Books, 1960), pp. 14-16.

2. George Santayana, "The Genteel Tradition in American Philosophy," an address delivered before the Philosophical Union of the University of California, August 25, 1911, reprinted in The Development of American Philosophy, by Walter G. Muelder and Laurence Sears (New York: Houghton Mifflin, Co., 1940), pp. 179-190.

3. Richard Rorty, "Pragmatism, Relativism and Irrationalism," Presidential Address, American Philosophical Association (Eastern Division), in Proceedings and Addresses of the American Philosophical Association (August 1980), 53:720. See also Morris Eames, Pragmatic Naturalism (Carbondale & Edwardsville: Southern Illinois University Press, 1979), pp. 22-23.

4. William James, Essays in Pragmatism, ed. Albury Castell (New York: Hafner Publishing Company, 1948), p. 36.

5. Rorty, Proceedings and Addresses, 53:719-720.

6. Immanuel Kant, Critique of Pure Reason, tr. Norman Kemp Smith (London: Macmillan, 1963), pp. 486-487.

7. William James, Some Problems of Philosophy: A Beginning of an Introduction to Philosophy (New York: Greenwood Press, 1968), p. 50.

8. Ibid.

9. Joseph Runzo, "James on Truth, Relativism and Religious Belief" (unpublished paper), p. 2.

10. William James, The Principles of Psychology, 2 vols. (New York: Dover Publications Inc., 1950), 1:609.

11. Ibid.

12. Ibid., 1:243.

13. Some Problems of Philosophy, p. 51.

14. Ibid., p. 53.

15. William James, The Meaning of Truth (Cambridge, Mass.: Harvard University Press, 1975), p. 119.

16. Bertrand Russell, Philosophical Essays (New York: Simon and Schuster, 1966), p. 105.

17. The Principles of Psychology, 1:221-222.

18. Ibid., 1:221.

19. J. Seelye Bixler, Religion in the Philosophy of William James (Boston: Marshall Jones Co., 1926), p. 21.

20. Anguttara-nikaya (abbr. A), ed. Richard Morris (London: Pali Text Society, 1961), 1:188-193.

21. Digha-nikaya (abbr. D), ed. T. W. Rhys Davids and J. E. Carpenter (London: Pali Text Society, 1967), 1:83-84.

22. Majjhima-nikaya (abbr. M), ed. V. Trenckner (London: Pali Text Society, 1948), 1:111-112.

23. David J. Kalupahana, Buddhist Philosophy: A Historical Analysis (Honolulu: The University Press of Hawaii, 1976), p. 21.

24. D 2:290-315; M 1:55-63.

25. D 2:290; M 1:55-56.

26. Svetasvatara Upanisad 1.3,15; see The Principal Upanisads, ed. & tr. S. Radhakrisnan (London: George Allen & Unwin, 1953), pp. 710, 717.

27. M 1:163-166.

28. D 1:292; M 1:56.

29. D 1:187.

David J. Kalupahana

30. Piyadassi Mahathera, Buddhist Meditation (15th Dona Alpina Ratnayaka Trust Lecture) (Kandy: Buddhist Publication Society, n.d.), p. 22.

31. D 1:79-83.

32. Ibid., 1:73.

33. A 5:2, 312, Iti kho bhikkhave kusalani silani anupubbena aggaya parenti.

34. Ian Stevenson, Twenty Cases Suggestive of Reincarnation (New York: 1966).

35. C. D. Broad, Human Personality and the Possibility of Its Survival (Berkeley & Los Angeles: University of California Press, 1955), p. 1.

36. Samyutta-nikaya (abbr. S), ed. L. Feer (London: Pali Text Society, 1960), 2:56-59.

37. Ibid.

38. Ibid., 2:26.

39. M 1:324.

40. S 2:25.

41. Ibid., 2:26.

42. Karl R. Popper and John C. Eccles, The Self and Its Brain (New York: Springer International, 1977), pp. 36-50.

43. D 1:83-84.

44. See Sutta-nipata, ed. Dines Anderson and Helmer Smith (London: Pali Text Society, 1913), vv. 425-449 (Padhana-sutta).

45. M 1:23.

46. Ibid., 1:167.

47. Essays in Pragmatism, p. 3.

48. Ludwig Wittgenstein, Tractatus Logico-Philosophicus, tr. D. F. Pears and B. F. McGuinness (London: Routledge & Kegan Paul), 1961, p. 5.

49. A 1:158-159.

50.   Ibid., 2:182-183.

51.   D 1:83.

52.   M 1:392-396.

53.   This is the essence of Chapter 1 ("On Skilfulness") of the Saddharmapundarika-sutra, which is expounded in Nagarjuna's Mulamadhyamakakarika, Chapter 24 ("On the Examination of the Four Noble Truths").

54.   M 2:212-213.

55.   William James, The Varieties of Religious Experience (New York: Macmillan, 1970), p. 392.

St. John of the Cross
on Mystic Apprehensions
as Sources of Knowledge
Nelson Pike

That mystic visions and locutions have value as potential
sources of information is a theme that is clearly detectable in
Augustine's Literal Commentary on Genesis and in that portion of
the Summa Theologica devoted to a discussion of what Aquinas
refers to as "Prophecy" (1). It is a view that governs thinking
about mystic apprehensions (2) in most modern manuals of Christian
mysticism as well. Further, that some of the information that has
been conveyed in this way consists of propositions of importance
to the Faith is, again, a commonplace thesis in the literature of
Christian mysticism. For example, when cataloging the kinds of
information that can be (as he says) "prophetically revealed," in
addition to descriptions of mundane facts revealed to Solomon
concerning the kinds of beasts and fishes indigenous to the lands
surrounding Israel, Aquinas lists some that (in his words)
"surpass human knowledge" such as the mystery of the Trinity which
was revealed in the vision of the Seraphim described in Isaiah II
(iv, 3). On this same topic, in Chapter 18 of what is perhaps the
most widely respected modern treatise on Christian mystical
theology, viz., The Graces of Interior Prayer, Anton Poulain
writes as follows concerning the vision of the Trinity that not
uncommonly accompanies the state of mystic contemplation called
"rapture":

> Even if we did not know by the Church's
> teaching how many persons there are in God,
> and how they proceed One from the Other, we
> should come to know it, and, by experience,
> through seeing it (in rapture) (3).

Remarks of a similar sort can be found in most of the classical as
well as modern texts that constitute the center of the Christian
mystical literature.

It is when viewed in the context of this tradition that the
renegade nature of the dominant thesis advanced by St. John of the
Cross in Book II of his celebrated work The Ascent of Mount Carmel
can best be appreciated. In this source, although there are
passages that suggest a contrary (i.e., more traditional) view
(4), John's principal claim seems clearly to be that the private
experiences of individual mystics have no value whatsoever as
sources of information. John insists on this point with respect
to the visions and locutions recorded in the Bible; and on the
question of whether the experiences of mystics can serve as a

75

basis for accepting truths already revealed to the Church (e.g., the mystery of the Trinity), John's remarks also carry a heavily negative verdict. Further, not only does John claim that mystic apprehensions are useless as information-bearers; his position is that to treat them as such is to risk a variety of pitfalls of considerable threat to the spiritual life. As regards the latter, before one can accept a given apprehension as a source of genuine knowledge, one must make what is traditionally referred to as a "discernment of spirits." This is to say that one must determine whether the apprehension is a communication from a reliable source (e.g., God) as opposed to an unreliable informant (e.g., the devil). And according to John, since this is an especially subtle and complicated task, the receiving mystic must be prepared to suffer not only the distraction of making the relevant calculations, but the anxiety that goes with the possibility of making a mistake. These disturbances, plus the fact that if error is made the mystic could be led to embrace a false belief injurious to his faith, is what makes the project precarious in the extreme (5). But, of course, in spite of the dangers, one must allow that in some cases the visionary will succeed in discovering that his vision is from a reliable source and thus can be trusted to convey only truth. The center of St. John's negative stance regarding the epistemic value of mystic apprehensions is that even in this optimal case, the apprehension in question cannot be taken as a legitimate source of propositional knowledge. It is with respect to this last thesis that John parts company with virtually the whole of the classical as well as modern Christian theological opinion on this topic. It is this that leads him to declare in the end that mystics ought not to busy themselves with the discernment of spirits. With respect to apprehensions generally, one ought not to seek them nor (once given) "accept them or keep them." John says that whether they be true visions or false, the best thing to do is to "reject them all" (6).

In the first two sections of the present paper, I review and then critique a theory concerning the nature of mystic apprehensions that is advanced by St. John in Book II, Chapters 18-20 of the Ascent and that has as a consequence the negative thesis just identified. Section three is then offered as an expansionary interlude in which attention is focused on an account proposed by the contemporary Protestant theologian Emil Brunner of what he calls "the revelation in creation." I argue that although Brunner's theory of revelation differs importantly from the one formulated by St. John in Chapters 18-20, both embody the same incoherent theological thesis. The point of the interlude is to display this thesis in its most general form. This is done by first identifying and then discounting variations in its content as it appears in the two contexts studied. In the fourth and final section of the paper I return to Book II of the Ascent in an effort to piece together a second argument for John's negative position on the epistemic value of mystic apprehensions that does

not make use of the deficient thesis inherent in the first. I
should add that the argument developed in this concluding section
rests on a theory concerning the nature of mystic apprehensions
that is constructed, rather than simply lifted out of John's
remarks on this subject. Though much of the relevant material is
taken from Chapter 17, essential ingredients are imported from
scattered discussions in later portions of the text - in
particular, from Chapters 21, 22, 24, 27, and 29. For this
reason, some may protest that the theory suggested is, at best,
Sanjaunian rather than John's own view. Be this as it may (and I
shall leave this question for others to decide), I am anxious
that the theory be injected into the serious philosophical
discussion of mysticism that is just now getting under way. It is
one that has prompted me (at least) to re-think my presuppositions
regarding what we as students of the mystical literature should be
looking for when attempting to estimate the epistemic value of
mystic apprehensions or, for that matter, mystical experiences
more generally.

I. On the Meaning-Opacity of
Mystic Apprehensions

I can know that a given string of symbols expresses a
proposition, understand the proposition, but not know whether the
proposition in question is true. That is commonplace.
Correlatively, I can know that a given string of symbols expresses
a proposition, know that the proposition is true, but not
understand the proposition in question. This last is exemplified
by the case where Paul Revere is expecting a message from the bell
tower concerning the course of the British advance, but after
receiving the signal from his trusted comrade, realizes that he
never did have it straight whether it is one if by land and two if
by sea or two if by land and one if by sea. Here, Revere knows
that the glimmer from the tower is an information-bearer, knows
that the information contained in the message is true, but does
not know what the propositional content of the message is supposed
to be.

With this thought in mind, consider the case of Abraham who,
after being brought to the land of Canaan, was told by God: "I
will give you this land." Abraham was led to believe that he would
someday rule this land. Imagine his astonishment (as well as that
of those around him) when he found himself old and enfeebled
without ever having ruled in Canaan (7). What went wrong here?
The most obvious conclusion would appear to be that the message
contained in the words spoken to Abraham was false. However,
neither John nor any other traditional mystical theologian would
allow this as a possibility. Within the Christian mystical
community, it is held as an axiom that if a given mystic
apprehension is produced by God (is "from God" or is "divine")
whatever revelation (message) is contained in that apprehension is

true (8). Well, then, what did go wrong in the case of Abraham? John claims that in this case the revelation contained in the divine locution was not that Abraham, himself, would rule in Canaan, but that Abraham's descendants would possess that land someday in the distant future. Abraham simply misunderstood the words. He thus did not receive the message therein contained.

Using this and a number of other cases taken mostly from Old Testament sources (9), John arrives at the following general account: As a rule, when God attempts to communicate <u>via</u> direct verbal symbols (locutions), the words he employs are not used in their ordinary senses. There are passages in which John suggests that this is not just true as a general rule, but holds in every case (10). God speaks in a kind of code. Unlike Revere's comrade, however, the symbols God uses are the same as those used in everyday language. It is the meanings attached to the symbols that are different. It is thus not surprising that in some instances, even though the message contained in a given locution is true, because the words are taken literally they convey a message that is false. John maintains that there have been cases in which "the ideas (expressed) in God's words are so different from the meanings men would ordinarily derive from them," that even prophets such as Jeremiah and Christ's own disciples were led to hold false beliefs as a result of receiving divine communications (11).

Why should it be that when God communicates by way of locutions he uses words carrying meanings other than those attached to them when used by men in ordinary discourse? On John's account, the answer to this question has something to do with the nature of the messages God attempts to communicate. He says:

> God's chief objective in conferring these revelations is to express and impart the elusive spiritual meaning contained in the words. This spiritual meaning is richer and more plentiful than the literal meaning and transcends those limits (12).

Apparently ordinary language is simply not an adequate tool for expressing the "elusive spiritual meanings" that God wants to impart. In some passages John says that these meanings are simply not available to our understanding. The truths expressed are "hidden truths" that are quite beyond our powers of comprehension (13). However, there are other passages in which this position is softened. Sometimes John says that the meanings in question can never be <u>completely</u> comprehended - suggesting, perhaps, that they may be understood in part (14). At other times he tells us that the meanings expressed in the words used by God are only very difficult to understand - implying (I should think) that there is nothing here that is incomprehensible, but only meanings that we must work very hard to grasp (15). But whether John is claiming that the meanings expressed in the words used by God are incomprehensible, only partially comprehensible or just very difficult to understand, he seems clearly to be saying that they cannot be expressed in sentences using words carrying the meanings they have in ordinary human discourse (16).

If God's messages are coded, how shall we proceed when trying to uncover the revelation contained in a particular locution? John holds that there is no code-book, no translation-formula. There simply is no safe procedure by which one can begin with an understanding of the literal meaning of the words and emerge in the end with an understanding of the message therein contained. John writes:

> Let it be realized, therefore, that there is no complete understanding of the meanings of the sayings and things of God, and that this meaning cannot be decided by what it seems to be without great error and, in the end, grievous confusion (17).

The conclusion is that with respect to any given divine locution, one can never be sure that one has grasped the message carried by the words:

> Evidently, then, even though the words and revelations be from God, we cannot find assurance in them, since in our understanding of them we can easily be deluded and extremely so. They embody an abyss and depth of spiritual significance and to want to limit them to our interpretation and sensory apprehension is like wanting to grasp a handful of air, which will escape the hand entirely and leave only a particle of dust (18).

Up to this point, we have dealt exclusively with experiences in which words are apprehended (locutions) and have as yet said nothing about visual experiences (visions) which may or may not be accompanied by locutions. However, it is clear in John's text that he intends the conclusion just reached to apply to visions as well as to divine locutions. In the opening paragraphs of both Chapters 19 and 20 he claims that although the messages contained in both locutions and visions from God are true, in no case can one assume that one understands the messages in question. Why? In the case of locutions, the explanation rests in the fact that God uses words in extraordinary senses. But, of course, this explanation will not apply to visions where there are no verbal symbols and thus no ordinary or extraordinary senses of words to consider. Since John nowhere addresses himself separately to visions, there is something of an hiatus in the reasoning. Let me

here risk a suggestion as to how the argument might be completed.
Let us suppose that a small angel appears bolding a spear
with a hot iron tip (19). Let's assume that the apprehension is
from God and that it is a meaning-bearer that contains a message
having a positive truth value. What is the message, i.e., what is
the revelation contained in the vision? Even if one assumes that
there is one and only one such revelation, the question remains as
to what the specific content of that revelation is. I think that
what John would say is that there just is no way to answer this
question. Though we assume that the various elements of the
visual presentation (the size of the angel, the hot iron tip of
the spear, etc.) are symbols that jointly embody some
propositional message, there is no way to be sure that whatever
meaning we assign to it is the one that is actually intended.
There is no way to start with the symbols and arrive at the
meaning they presumably contain.

The upshot is, then, that neither divine locutions nor divine
visions can be taken as sources of knowledge - neither religious
knowledge such as that codified in the doctrines of the Church
(the mystery of the Trinity) nor mundane knowledge concerning,
e.g., the beasts and fishes indigenous to the lands surrounding
Israel. And what I think is most interesting here is not that
this conclusion is urged by one of the most important spokesmen
for the Christian mystical tradition (a fact already surprising in
the extreme), but that the argument for his negative position
proceeds without challenging any of the epistemic apparatus
standardly used in Christian mystical sources for determining the
reliability of mystic apprehensions (20). Since, for John,
whatever message is contained in a divine apprehension is (by
hypothesis) true, the issue here has nothing to do with lack of
assurance concerning reliability. John's claim is that even if we
grant that the message is true (since the apprehension is divine),
there is no safe way to determine precisely what it is. Mystic
apprehensions are, we might say, opaque as regards their meaning.
It is this that renders them useless as potential sources of
propositional knowledge.

II. Critique

The conclusion just reached concerning the meaning-opacity of
mystic apprehensions is presumably based on a study of Biblical
cases in which God (allegedly) tried to communicate truths to
selected individuals and because the truths in question were deep
(at best, very difficult for us to understand), God found it
necessary to formulate them in symbols carrying meanings other
than the ones they have in ordinary discourse. Because the
recipients interpreted the symbols in standard fashion, they
failed to receive the intended message. However, let's look again
at these Biblical cases. John tells us that the real message

intended for Abraham in the words "I will give you this land" was "I will give this land to your descendants." John identifies the precise nature of Abraham's mistake by identifying and then comparing the real message with the apparent message. This pattern is repeated when dealing with each of the cases treated in the text. But what is so difficult to understand about the sentence "I will give this land to your descendants"? This looks straightforward enough. Indeed, it is only because we can readily understand it that we can readily understand John's analysis of Abraham's mistake. Had the import of the real message been as opaque as John's conclusion would lead us to believe, we (and he) should have had difficulty understanding it and thus should have had equal difficulty understanding what John was telling us about the nature of Abraham's mistake. And note, too, John has apparently formulated the real message contained in the divine locution using only standard words carrying their ordinary meanings. If John were not using the words "I will give this land to your descendants" with standard meanings attached, since he provides no glossary to which we might refer, he could not assume that we would understand the real message and thus could not assume that we would understand the point he is making when identifying the specific nature of Abraham's mistake. Thus the cases used by John to support his generalization about the meaning-opacity of mystic locutions does nothing to warrant his final conclusion. If anything, they pull in the opposite direction: They look more like counter-examples than like cases meant to support his position.

This criticism seems to me to be decisive. However, what it is decisive against is not John's position concerning the meaning-opacity of divine apprehensions, but the procedure he uses when attempting to show that that position is correct. It is one of those special cases where the import of the theory undermines the argument used in its support. In the next few pages following, I want to argue that from the point of view of one committed to a more or less standard medieval picture of the nature of God, there is something wrong with the theory itself and not just with John's particular way of supporting it. I offer the argument to follow as one that might be advanced by, e.g., Thomas Aquinas in response to John's challenge of the traditional view concerning the epistemic value of mystic apprehensions.

God is omnipotent if he has unlimited productive power, i.e., if he has productive power greater than which cannot be conceived, i.e., if it is within God's power to bring about any state of affairs (S) where "God brings about S" describes a logical possibility. Secondly, God is omniscient if he knows all things knowable. Following Aquinas, the class of things knowable includes future events and circumstances, i.e., so-called "future contingents"(21). Lastly, allow that God counts as having communicated a given proposition (R) to a particular person (P) if God brings it about that P understands R. Now, with these three assumptions in mind, suppose that God exists and is both omnipotent and omniscient. I want to consider a case in which a person P does not understand a proposition R. And with respect to this case, there would appear to be three possibilities vis-a-vis God and his communicative activities, viz., (1) it was not possible for God to communicate R to P; (2) though it was possible for God to communicate R to P, God made no effort to do so; and (3) though it was possible for God to communicate R to P and God made an effort to do so, that attempt failed. I'll look at each of these three possibilities separately.

I'm not sure I can provide a really convincing illustration of the first possibility but, perhaps, the following will at least suggest how one might look. R is the Special Theory of Relativity and P is a severely retarded person suffering from Down's Syndrome. R is thus such as to be beyond the range of P's powers of comprehension and our notion of personal identity is such that any person having powers of comprehension sufficient for understanding R would fail to count as the person P. But, of course, if it were not possible for P to understand R, God (being omniscient) would know this. That P should be brought to understand R would then not be something that God might try to do. One can be described as trying to communicate R to P only if one undertakes an action that one knows, thinks, or at least suspects will, or at least might (so far as one knows to the contrary) bring it about that P understands R. But if God knew that it was not possible for P for understand R, he would also know that any action he might undertake to communicate R to P would fail to do so. Hence, in this circumstance God could not be described as having tried to communicate R to P. This is because in this circumstance, God could not be described as having undertaken an action that he knew, thought or even suspected would, or even might (so far as he knew to the contrary) bring it about that P understands R. If we assume alternative #1, therefore, it would appear that God could not have tried to commuicate R to P. Alternative #1 and alternative #2 thus seem to collapse into a single case, viz., one in which God made no attempt to communicate R to P. With respect to some person who does not understand a given proposition, therefore, our options concerning God's communicative activities reduce to two. Either God made no attempt to communicate R to P, or God made such an attempt and the attempt in question failed.

Consider a case in which it was possible for God to communicate R to P, God (allegedly) made an effort to do so, but the attempt failed. Let's suppose that the means of communication employed was a mystic locution or vision. Since it was possible for God to communicate R to P, we must assume that some other means of communication at God's disposal would have succeeded had it been employed. But God, being omniscient, would have known that the means of communication chosen was going to fail. He would also have known that some other means of communication would have succeeded. Under these conditions, the conclusion would again appear to be that God did nothing that would count as an attempt to communicate R to P. As suggested above, one makes an attempt to communicate a given proposition to a given person only if one undertakes an action that one knows, believes or at least suspects will, or at least might (so far as one knows to the contrary) result in that person understanding the proposition in question. But in the case before us, God undertook an action that He knew would not - and thus could not even have suspected that it might - result in P understanding R. This, by itself, is enough to assure that God made no effort to communicate R to P. This conclusion is reinforced when it is added that God specifically opted against some alternative mode of communication that He knew would have resulted in P understanding R. Alternative #3 thus appears to be incoherent. If a particular person fails to understand a given proposition, this cannot be because God tried but failed to communicate that proposition to the person in question.

At this point, a note of clarification should be added.

According to St. Thomas, an act of assent involves choice. The act of accepting a revelation from God thus involves an act of will on the part of the one receiving the revelation (22). If we now assume that the intelligent agents to whom revelations are given have free will, I could imagine someone arguing as follows: It makes perfectly good sense to suppose that God might try to get P to accept R and that that attempt might fail. P does not count as having accepted R unless he does so freely. Thus God could not make P accept R. To do so would involve making P do something freely. Of course, P does not count as having done something freely if he is made to do it by another. Hence, God can invite, command or demand that P accept R. He might also want or hope and thus encourage or cajole P to accept R. But these efforts might fail. P might reject R regardless of how persistent and skilled God's efforts to the contrary might be.

I cite this argument in order to make clear the following point of contrast.

Whatever connections there may be between the concept of assent and the concept of choice, understanding does not appear to be something one can choose (not choose, choose not) to do. I can choose (not choose, choose not) to take steps that lead (or may lead) to understanding. I can thus choose (not choose, choose not) to bring myself to a point where understanding occurs. But understanding itself seems best described not in the language of action, but in the language of occurrences, happenings or events. Thus, even if one grants that God could not make a given individual assent to a given proposition (on the grounds that assent requires an act of choice), I see no reason to deny that God could effect the corresponding case of understanding. So far as I can see, the claim that God might try but fail to communicate a given proposition to a given individual can receive no shelter by appeal to the peculiarities of the notion of choice. Given that God is both omnipotent and omniscient, any communicative effort he makes must, of necessity, succeed.

III. Expansion

According to Emil Brunner in Revelation and Reason (23), the reason why God created the universe was to provide a "manifestation of His (own) power and wisdom" and thus to reveal Himself to rational creatures (24). Brunner elaborates this idea as follows:

> God's will and nature are such that He creates in order to reveal himself. That which is created bears the stamp of its Maker through His will as Creator and through His act of creation. Therefore, the doctrine of analogia entis, which has been such a controversial topic of late, is not peculiar to the Catholic Church, but it has been part of the common Christian inheritance of belief from the earliest days of the Church; for it simply expresses the fact that it has pleased God so to create the world that in and through it His "everlasting power and divinity" may be made known (25).

Brunner makes clear that this is a comment about what he calls the "objective process of revelation," i.e., about the content communicated as well as the means employed by the one whose intention it is to communicate. Concerning the other side of the equation, i.e., "the subjective reception of the revelation on the part of man," Brunner comments so:

> The works of God in creation are placed before the eyes of all, and reason is the endowment common to all men, and that which places them on a higher plane than that occupied by all other creatures. The objective process of revelation, or the objective means of revelation, and the subjective capacity to receive the revelation are thus made for each other (26).

But, given this much, a question must surely arise about why it is that not all men have received the message contained in the divine revelatory act of creation. Brunner replies that this is because of the corruption inherent in man's sinful nature. The idea that man is a sinner is not just the idea that man is corrupt in "heart and will." Brunner insists that...

> ...it is an integral part of the sin of man that the knowledge of God which begins to dawn

upon him through revelation is suppressed by
him, so that the revelation which God gives
him for knowledge of Himself becomes the
source of the vanity of idolatry. God gives
the revelation in order that man may know Him,
but man turns this into an illusion (27).

Shall we then conclude that the divine act of creation is not an
act of communication after all? Brunner says:

As the Bible, just as it is, is an objective
means of God's revelation - whether men
understand it as God's word or not - so also
the creation is a means of divine revelation
whether men see it as such or not (28).

The point is that although God's self-disclosure in the act of
creation is (in Brunner's words) "communicated to" (29) and is
"meant" (30) or "intended" (31) for all men, man is afflicted with
an "incomprehensible blindness" (32) which prevents detection of
what Brunner refers to as "the meaning" (33) of God's revelation.
Using a variation on the analogy introduced in the first section
of this essay, we can say that the message is being beamed from
the tower and the receiving equipment (reason) has been amply
provided. The problem is that the equipment has fallen into
disrepair. Brunner concludes:

The result is that man either does not
perceive this evident, divine revelation, or,
if he thinks he perceives it, he falls into
gross error and misunderstanding (34).

Regarding the credentials of the position just reviewed,
Brunner says that it is a doctrine very clearly advanced in the
works of the Reformers (principally Calvin) and is also in harmony
with the teachings of the Bible. In both sources (Brunner assures
us) we find insistence on the truth of the message contained in
what he calls "the general revelation" or "the revelation in
creation" coupled with the claim that there can be no "natural
knowledge of God," i.e., that natural theology is not a
possibility. Brunner insists that in both sources, too, the
explanation of this somewhat surprising circumstance rests on the
recognition of (in Brunner's words):

...the cognitive significance of sin, that is,
the fact that it prevents the knowledge of
God. As one who <u>knows</u>, man stands in just as
much opposition to the truth of God as he does
in the sphere of action; his knowledge is no
better than his practical relation to God; his
knowledge is as corrupt as his heart (35).

85

Brunner makes clear that the act of creation is only one of several "forms" or "methods" that God employs when attempting to communicate knowledge to men. Another, of course, is the Bible and there will be yet a third used in the final days (36). Thus, I do not want to suggest that what I have just reviewed is the whole or even a major part of what Brunner has to say about God's revelation to men. However, I have enough for present purposes. I now want to return to the theory advanced by St. John to note some points of comparison.

A difference between Brunner and John regarding the vehicle by which revelation is conveyed is obvious. For Brunner it is the whole of creation while for John the message is contained in more localized phenomena such as words spoken on a specific occasion. However, more interesting differences are to be found in what Brunner and John have to say about the content of revelation, i.e., about what it is that God attempts to convey via whatever vehicle is involved. First, let me say that I have not been able to discover whether or not for Brunner we are to think of the content of the revelation in creation as a piece of information that is (or might be) cast in propositional form, e.g., that God is wise and powerful or that the creator of the universe is wise and powerful. The fact that Brunner speaks of God's message as being available to reason and makes clear that he is (at least in part) concerned in this portion of the text with the question of whether natural theology is a real possibility, would suggest that the revelatory content is propositional. Still, when talking about the revelation contained in the Bible, Brunner insists that the relevant content is God Himself and not information of one sort or another (37). Exactly what this means and whether it is intended to hold for the "revelation in creation" as well as the Biblical revelation is not very easy to tell. However this may be (and I shall not pursue it further), for Brunner the content (whether propositional or otherwise) appears to be singular (God's power and wisdom), is projected in a single communicative action (the act of creation), and is intended for a multiple audience consisting of all human beings. For John, on the other hand, what is revealed (clearly propositional in nature) consists of separate messages, separately delivered to each of a number of specifically targeted receivers. From an epistemological point of view, however, a further difference would appear to be more salient than any of these. According to Brunner, the meaning that God attempts to communicate by way of the act of creation is "manifest" and "evident" and is also readily available to man's natural powers of comprehension. Recall that on this last point, he insists that the "objective" elements (the message and the means of communication) and the "subjective" element (man's capacity to receive the message) are well-coordinated, (in his words) "made for each other." Thus on Brunner's theory, the fact that men fail to grasp the meaning contained in the divine communication cannot be traced to some feature of the message, the medium or the natural receiving equipment. For him, the trouble is located in a

kind of maintenance failure: the receiving apparatus has fallen
into a deplorable state of corrosion. All of this stands in
contrast with the explanation offered by John. For him the
communication failure stems from the fact that the messages
involved are not well-suited to man's natural intellectual
capabilities and thus cannot be framed in the language men use to
communicate thoughts to one another. God must then resort to a
code. Communicative failure results when the code is misunderstood
by the intended receivers.

Though these differences are interesting, I have stressed
them not for their own sake but in order to isolate a thesis that
is common to the theories advanced by Brunner and John and in
relation to which each can be seen as a variation on a theme. The
thesis in question is this:

> God attempts to communicate something or other
> ( ) to some one or more of his intelligent
> creatures ( ) but for one reason or another
> God's attempts to communicate   to   does not
> succeed.

I argued above that given a standard medieval theological context
in which God is held to be omnipotent as well omniscient and in
which the doctrine of divine omniscience is held to entail
foreknowledge of future contingents, the reasoning John offers in
support of his negative position concerning the epistemic value of
mystic apprehensions is incoherent. What I now want to suggest is
that in any theological system that includes these same doctrinal
elements (and this would include those of Brunner and Calvin)
(38), any argument utilizing some version of the general thesis
just formulated will be incoherent as well. As a general
principle, God succeeds in communicating whatever it is that he
attempts to communicate. So far as I can see, the theological
assumptions operating in our discussion simply will not tolerate
the contrary view.

IV. Illumination

If what I have said in the preceding two sections is right,
John's theory concerning the epistemic value of mystic
apprehensions involves two incompatible claims, viz., (1) God's
purpose (intention, objective) in conferring mystic apprehensions
is to convey information to selected receivers; and (2) mystic
apprehensions have no value as information-bearers. Of course, it
is the second of these that constitutes John's stand against
mainstream theological opinion on this topic. The first is
strictly in accord with traditional thinking as evidenced in the
writings of Augustine and Aquinas. Framed in the light of this
last observation, my criticism of John's theory might be put as

follows: John rejects part, but he also accepts part of the traditional account. The trouble is that the part that John accepts entails the part that he rejects. The upshot is that John's theory as a whole is pulled between two incompatible poles. Considerations of consistency would thus suggest that John make a choice. Either he can retreat from the contra-traditional position expressed in #2 above, or he can depart the tradition even more severely than he already has and deny the claim formulated in #1. John must either go the distance or return to the fold: the half-way house simply is not viable. In what is to follow, I shall be focused on a theme running through much of the discussion in Book II of the Ascent that involves the denial of #1, i.e., that centers on the idea that God provides mystic apprehensions for purposes other than that of conveying information. This is the theme of major concern in the present paper. In my opinion, it not only furnishes a consistent ground for his negative theory concerning the epistemic value of mystic apprehensions (i.e., #2); it is also the most provocative of John's many interesting reflections on this general topic.

Speaking of apprehensions that are produced by God, in Sec. 6 of Chapter 24, John says this:

> The effects these visions produce in the soul
> are: quietude, illumination, gladness
> resembling that of glory, delight, purity,
> love, humility, and an elevation and
> inclination toward God. Sometimes these
> effects are more intense, sometimes less. The
> diversity is due to the spirit that receives
> them and to God's wishes.

Mystic apprehensions that are produced by the devil (or one of his henchpeople) can be used for clarifying contrast. In the next section of the same chapter, John describes them so:

> The devil's visions produce spiritual dryness
> in one's communications with God and an
> inclination to self-esteem to admiring them
> and to considering them important. In no way
> do they cause mildness of humility and love of
> God...The memory of them is considerably arid
> and unproductive of the love and humility
> caused by the remembrance of good visions.

Teresa of Avila said much this same thing in various passages sprinkled through her writings. On her account, divine apprehensions usually result in happiness, joy and a sense of peace. Even if fraught with pain and remorse, they result in a sense of humility, a sense of one's own sinfulness, an inclination toward virtue and an awareness of one's own need for God. Teresa emphasized, too, that daemonic visions and locutions have precisely the opposite effects. One so afflicted is "...troubled, disturbed and restless; (one) loses that devotion and joy (that one) previously had and cannot pray at all" (39).

Note, first of all, that relative to that of the preceding discussion, the focus of attention has changed. Above, when dealing with a given apprehension, the generative question was "what does it mean?" Here, we are no longer asking "what does it mean?" but, rather, "what does it cause?", i.e., what effects does it have primarily as regards the production of certain attitudes, feeling states and behavioral dispositions on the part of the receiving individual visionary. Of course, the answer we are given differs depending on whether the relevant apprehension is of the divine or daemonic variety. But note, secondly, that the answer given in each case does not presuppose that the visionary has somehow arrived at a correct understanding of something called "the meaning" of the apprehension. John makes clear that any effects produced by a given apprehension are produced quite independently of any effort made on the part of the visionary to understand it (40). With this thought in mind, we can immediately identify a clear value that attaches to divine apprehensions whether or not they are effective as meaning-bearers. Visions and locutions from God are causally efficacious as regards a range of attitudes, feeling states and behavioral dispositions that facilitate what John refers to as "spiritual growth" of the receiving mystic (41). They work on the soul as a dose of vitamins might work on the body. They effect a kind of spiritual tune-up that results in easy commerce between the visionary and God. Question: Why does God confer mystic apprehensions? Answer: In spite of the danger of error and confusion, they are given in order to enhance the "spiritual growth" of the individual receiver.

This answer seems to me to signal a promising turn in the discussion. However, if we were to leave it at that, while divine apprehensions would then be portrayed as having value for the spiritual life, we would have no reason to think of them as having anything identifiable as cognitive, i.e., epistemic value since the benefits so far mentioned have only to do with what might be called "conative" factors such as the occurrence of certain attitudes, feeling states and behavioral dispositions. This would omit from consideration one of the themes running through John's discussion, viz., that divine apprehensions are vehicles by which (as he says) "the spirit is instructed" (42). They are means by which the individual visionary receives a special kind of knowledge - something that John describes as "supreme knowledge" and that he refers to alternatively as "spiritual wisdom" and "illumination" (43). Making use of an example of my own, I now want to suggest a way of understanding this idea that keeps us on the track we are already on but which introduces a reason why God confers apprehensions that relates to the cognitive side of the spiritual life. It also allows additional perspective as to why John is as firm as he is when advising against the traditional way of understanding the potential epistemic value of mystic visions and locutions.

I have in mind a man whose mother died when he was a boy. Some of his memories of her are vivid but most are very dim. Partly because he can remember some of the relevant events, but mostly because he was told by others long after her death, he knows that his mother had a very special attachment to him as a child. As an adult, the man has a dream. In the dream he is a boy again, running up the walk on his way home from school. He stumbles and bruises his knee. Looking up he sees his mother bending over him wearing a brightly colored scarf. He hears her say: "There, there, my little boy." He feels the peace of her presence. The dreamer then awakens and finds himself thinking "My mother loved me deeply." Of course, that is something that he had known for years, but I am supposing a case in which via the dream, something new is added. There is a distinction between just knowing something and really getting it, i.e., between correctly believing with evidence and grasping something at the base of the mind as something more than just correct information. That which was only known before now resonates more as a kind of cognitive-feeling than as an ordinary thought. The new understanding - the depth grasp - that is what I want here to suppose has been added in this case.

I have three comments to make about the case described in this story. As I proceed, I shall weave in some of John's remarks concerning the way we should think about mystic apprehensions.

First, if a question were to arise about the evidence the dreamer has for thinking that his mother loved him deeply, it would consist of what he remembers from his childhood together with what he had been told over the years by others in a position to know. These are the reasons the dreamer has for thinking that what he believes about his mother is true. Further, it is clear, I think, that whatever else might be said about the epistemic relevance of the dream I have described, it could not be included in the list. One does not verify a proposition about the affections of his mother by citing the content of a dream-experience. Even in the case where what one dreams is true, or what one dreams prompts an investigation that later yields knowledge, that it is true or that it is knowledge cannot be supported by pointing to the fact that is was dreamed. The point here is that unlike ordinary, waking-life visual or auditory experiences, we simply do not accept a dream-experience as a legitimate source of knowledge.

Claiming first that there are no more articles of the Faith to be revealed to the Church, in Book II, Chapter 27, Sec. 4 of the Ascent John comments as follows on revelations of religious truths received via mystic apprehensions:

> In order to preserve the purity of his faith,
> a person should not believe already revealed
> truths because they are again revealed, but

because they were already sufficiently
revealed to the Church. Closing his mind to
them, he should rest simply on the doctrine of
the Church and its faith which, as St. Paul
says, enters through the hearing (Rom. 10:17).
And if he wants to escape delusion, he should
not adapt this credence and intellect to those
truths revealed again, no matter how true and
conformed to the faith they may seem (44).

John is saying that a mystic apprehension ought not to be taken as
a reliable source of religious information. Even in the case
where what is revealed in the apprehension is true, it ought not
to be believed <u>because</u> it is given in the apprehension, but
because it is an item of faith already specified in Church
doctrine. The issue here does not concern what is believed, but
what is to count as a legitimate ground for believing it. In this
regard, a mystic apprehension is like a dream-experience.
Whatever its specific content may be, it cannot be cited as a
reason for thinking that what one believes is true.

Returning to the dream, let us ask, secondly, why it was that
the dreamer came away from the dream harbouring the specific idea
that his mother loved him deeply. After all, in the dream his
mother didn't actually say that. All she said was "There, there,
my little boy." Then perhaps the proposition "My mother loved me
deeply" was somehow deciphered from the visual content - the look
on his mother's face or the scarf around her neck. But how can
the dreamer be sure that his "translation" of these sensible
images is correct? Where is the codebook? What do these things
really mean? I'll pause here for a moment to explain why I think
that this inquiry is irrelevant.

Suppose that after awakening, the dreamer in my story had
assumed that the dream was a vehicle by which some message was
being communicated to him - by God, by his mother, or perhaps by
the local telepathist who tends to be something of a prankster.
He then sets out to determine the message. Treating the auditory
and visual dream-content as symbols, he assigns them a meaning and
arrives at the message for the dream. <u>Now</u> we can raise the
sceptical questions posed above. They point to the fact that in
the scenario just sketched, the dream contents were treated as
data subject to something that would count as an <u>interpretation</u>.
But this is not the case I meant to be describing in the original
story. In the latter, while the dream was described as having
cognitive impact, I purposely omitted an interval in the telling
where the dreamer busied himself with the intellectual occupation
of deciphering symbols. In my case, the dream is not treated as a
communication subject to interpretation. If it is a communication
at all (and I would not want to exclude this as a possibility), it
works more like a piece of subliminal advertising than like a
James Joyce novel. What I mean to be emphasizing here is that in
the case as I intend it, the relationship between the dream and

the cognitive state that results is <u>causal</u>. What is important, then, is not whether the <u>dream</u> is properly understood. So long as <u>via</u> the dream the dreamer comes to understand <u>that</u> <u>his</u> <u>mother</u> <u>loved</u> <u>him</u> <u>deeply</u>, the case remains the same for my purposes even if it be added that the dream itself is not understood at all.

This leads to a more general observation: In the case we have been discussing, the dreamer dreamed about his mother. It was she whom he saw bending over him; it was she who said: "There, there, my little boy." Appropriately enough, the cognitive state that the dream occasioned was also about his mother - what he came to understand was that his mother loved him deeply. But given the remarks made in the preceding paragraph, one can see, I think, that this coincidence of content was in no way essential to the case. We could have imagined a case in which the dreamer dreamed a sequence in which he saw only the homestead and heard only a low melodious hum coming from the kitchen. He might still awake with a depth-realization that he expresses in the sentence: "My mother loved me deeply." In the same way, we could imagine a case in which the auditory and visual content of the dream was as it was in the one described, but in which the dreamer awoke from the dream-experience harbouring a very different cognitive-feeling - perhaps one that he expresses in the sentence: "My father did not love my mother," or in the sentence: "Honey is sweeter than wine." If there are regularities here (and I suppose that there are) they will not be captured in translation rules - rules that tell us how to "read" symbols or how otherwise to determine something called "the meaning" of a dream. What rules there are will be (broadly) causal principles - perhaps principles of association or something of the sort.

In Book II, Chapter 26 of the <u>Ascent</u>, John discusses the specific kinds of "knowledge" communicated to the individual visionary by way of (so-called) "intellectual" visions and locutions. In Sec. 16 he makes the following general comment about these knowledge states as well as those obtained from other kinds of divine apprehensions:

> These kinds of knowledge, as well as the other, come to the soul passively, and thereby exclude any active endeavor of the soul. For it will happen that, while a person is distracted and inattentive, a keen understanding of what he is hearing or reading will be implanted in his spirit, an understanding far clearer than that conveyed through the sound of words. And although sometimes he fails to grasp the sense of the words - as when expressed in Latin, a language unknown to him - this meaning is revealed without his understanding the words themselves.

The "keen understanding" (as John calls it) is "implanted" via the
apprehension quite independently of any effort made on the part of
the visionary. In particular, the keen understanding does not
result from any effort made on the part of the receiver to
interpret the visual or auditory materials making up the
apprehension. Is it Latin? No matter that one can't understand
it. What is understood is understood by way of the apprehension.
This can happen even if whatever it is that one hears or sees is
not, itself, understood. The point, I think, is that although the
apprehension is here being thought of as a means of communication,
the relationship between the vehicle and the message delivered is
causal. In this respect, then, the cognitive value of a given
apprehension is on precisely the same footing with what I referred
to earlier as the "conative" benefits. Like the latter, the
former are what John calls "effects" that come to the individual
"passively" and are "fixed in the soul without its having need for
effort of its own" (45). We can see, then, that the auditory or
visual content of the apprehension is of no special importance.
What is important is the cognitive-state that is causally
effected. The content of the latter may or may not coincide with
what is actually heard or seen in the apprehension itself.
     Thirdly, and lastly, go back for a moment to the reasons John
gives for advising that mystic apprehensions be greeted by the
visionary with an air of intellectual indifference, even
rejection. When they are given, one ought not to bother
deciphering them. Regardless of how keen the "keen understanding"
they afford may be, they ought not to be taken as a ground for
religious conviction (46). If I am right in my estimate of how
John is thinking about the way in which divine apprehensions are
intended to work, these maxims make a lot of sense. In the case
of a dream, why set about to determine what it means? In the
first place, that would require a lot of energy that might better
be used elsewhere. In the second place, since there are no
translation rules with which to work, it can't be done. In the
third place, if you try to do it and take the results seriously,
you may make a mistake and thus be led to embrace a false belief.
And in the fourth place, if you try to do it and take the results
seriously, even if you are not led to embrace a false belief, you
will be deceived if you think (as you likely will) that you have
thereby added to your store of knowledge. Of course, this is not
to say that a mystic apprehension is devoid of interest for the
epistemologist. It, like a dream, can have an important effect on
what might be called the "mode," rather than the content of the
knowledge state. The point is, however, that like a dream, it
ought not to be thought of as an information-bearer. What
epistemic value it has comes in the form of a cognitive-wallop
rather than in the form of a proposition.

Postscript

John's cognitive-wallop theory of mystic apprehensions requires the assumption that there is a body of truth to which the individual mystic has access by means other than mystic visions and locutions. Without this assumption, John could not claim that the depth-understanding caused by an apprehension is the depth-understanding of a truth. And without this, it is hard to see how John could say that the mystic apprehension makes some contribution to something that would count as a knowledge-state of the experiencing mystic. John's specific version of the needed assumption consists of the claim that there is a body of truth that has been revealed to the Church - the one codified in Church doctrine. The individual mystic thus has access to the relevant truths not by way of mystic apprehensions but by the ordinary instructional devices used by the Church for disseminating doctrine. But what shall we say about the means by which the truths in question were originally revealed to the Church? Reference to the Bible and to the interpretative deliverances of various Church councils would no doubt be relevant. But what about these materials? Shall we suppose that the truths involved were revealed by God to certain individuals, e.g., those who composed the books of the Bible, individual members of the various Church councils, or the Pope? And if we do suppose this, shall we then allow that the relevant divine communications were mystic apprehensions such as the one given to Abraham? But, of course, that wouldn't do. According to John's theory, mystic apprehensions cannot be taken as a source of propositional knowledge. Their function presupposes that the receiver is already in possession of the truths to which they relate. Is this a difficulty for John? I'm not sure - I haven't thought it though far enough to tell. But whether or not it turns out to be a difficulty for the theory, John's cognitive-wallop analysis of visions and locutions presupposes a view concerning the origin of what John sometimes calls the "Public Revelation" that does not depend on the idea that it was delivered by God to individual receivers via anything classifiable as a mystic apprehension. John's finished mystical theology will require an account of the Public Revelation that does not derive it from God-given visions or locutions (47).

NOTES

1. Pt. II-II, Q. 171-174.

2. The term "apprehension" is used by John to cover both visions and locutions. As a general remark, visions are visual or visual-like experiences while locutions are auditory or auditory-like experiences. (Cf. Ascent of Mount Carmel, II, Ch. 23, Sec. 3.) Within the Christian mystical tradition, apprehensions constitute one of two broad classes of mystical experiences and are usually referred to as "Gratuitous Graces" (i.e., special gifts from God). The other broad class of mystical experiences is referred to as the "states of infused contemplation" or, more colloquially, the "states of mystic union."

3. Ch. 18, no. par. 23. This passage taken from the 1910 English edition translated by Leonora York Smith (Kegan Paul, Trench Trubner and Co.)

4. Two passages in particular seem to fit this category, viz., Pt. II, Ch. 22, Secs. 2 and 3; and Ch. 26, Secs. 12 and 13.

5. Ascent, II, Ch. 17, Sec. 7. See also Ch. 16, Sec. 14; Ch. 21, Sec. 7; Ch. 29, Sec. 11; and Ch. 30, Sec. 5.

6. Ascent, II, Ch. 17, Secs. 6-9. Cf. also Ch. 16, Secs. 10-14.

7. Ascent, II, Ch. 19, Sec. 2.

8. Cf. Aquinas' Summa Theologica, II-II, Q. 171, a. 6. St. John concurs, e.g. Ascent, II, Ch. 19, Sec. 1 (first sentence); Ch. 19, Sec. 14; and Ch. 20, Sec. 1 (first sentence).

9. Some other cases given in Ascent II, Ch. 19 are these: (1) Sec. 3: Jacob is told by God that he should go to Egypt and that when the time comes, he (God) will lead him out again. Jacob dies in Egypt. Real message: God will lead Jacob's descendants out of Egypt. (2) Sec. 7: Jeremiah is told by God: "Peace will come to you." However, only wars and trials fall on Jeremiah and the people of Israel. Real message: The Messiah is coming sometime in the future. (3) Secs. 7-8: David is told by God that the Messiah will reign and free the people from bondage. The Messiah is born of humble state and is, himself, persecuted and slain by those who oppress Israel. Real message: Christ reigns in heaven and frees the people from the Devil. (4) Sec. 12: A devout man is told by God: "I will free you from your enemies." His enemies prevail against him and kill him. Real message: "I will give you salvation." (5) Sec. 13: A devout man who wants to be a martyr is told by God: "You shall be a martyr." He dies peacefully in his sleep. Real message: "I will give you the love and peace that

goes with being a martyr." I should point out that some of the cases that John cites in this connection are not of this form and do not support the generalization I am about to formulate. For example, Ch. 20, Sec. 1: Jonah is told by God that he will destroy the city of Ninive in 45 days. He does not. In the interim, the people repent and God does not follow through. In this case, it is not that Jonah misunderstood what he heard; it is, rather, that the condition "unless the people repent" was not explicit in the original formulation.

10. <u>Ascent</u>, II, Ch. 19, Secs. 5, 7, and 11.

11. <u>Ascent</u>, II, Ch. 19, Secs. 7 and 9.

12. <u>Ascent</u>, II, Ch. 19, Sec. 5. This passage and all others to be quoted in this paper from the <u>Ascent</u> are taken from the 1964 English edition translated by <u>Kieran</u> Kavanaugh and Otilio Rodriguez (New York: Doubleday). Cf. also Ch. 19, Sec. 1.

13. <u>Ascent</u>, II, Ch. 20, Sec. 5.

14. <u>Ascent</u>, II, Ch. 20, Sec. 6.

15. <u>Ascent</u>, II, Ch. 19, Sec. 7 (first line) and Sec. 9 (first line).

16. <u>Ascent</u>, II, Ch. 19, Secs. 5 and 11.

17. <u>Ascent</u>, II, Ch. 20, Sec. 6.

18. <u>Ascent</u>, II, Ch. 19, Sec. 10. Cf. also Ch. 18, Sec. 9; and Ch. 19, Sec. 1.

19. Such a vision was reported by St. Teresa of Avila in her <u>Life</u>, Ch. 29.

20. I review and discuss the elements of this apparatus in an article "Mystic Visions as Sources of Knowledge" which is printed in <u>Mysticism</u> <u>and</u> <u>Philosophical</u> <u>Analysis</u>, ed. Steven Katz (London: Sheldon Press, 1978).

21. <u>Summa</u> <u>Theologica</u>, I, Q. 14, a. 13.

22. <u>Summa</u> <u>Theologica</u>, II-II, Q. 2, a. 1 and 2.

23. <u>Revelation</u> <u>and</u> <u>Reason:</u> <u>The</u> <u>Christian</u> <u>Doctrine</u> <u>of</u> <u>Faith</u> <u>and</u> <u>Knowledge</u>, Zurick, 1941. All references to this text will be to the 1946 English edition translated by Olive Wyon (Reprinted by permission of The Westminster Press).

24. <u>Revelation</u> <u>and</u> <u>Reason</u>, p. 68.

25. Revelation and Reason, p. 67.

26. Revelation and Reason, p. 68.

27. Revelation and Reason, p. 65. See also p. 66.

28. Revelation and Reason, p. 68.

29. Revelation and Reason, pp. 63 and 67.

30. Revelation and Reason, p. 84.

31. Revelation and Reason, p. 84.

32. Revelation and Reason, p. 77.

33. Revelation and Reason, pp. 77 and 84.

34. Revelation and Reason, p. 68.

35. Revelation and Reason, p. 65.

36. Revelation and Reason, pp. 58-59.

37. Revelation and Reason, pp. 25ff.

38. It is interesting to note that in Book I, Ch. 6, Sec. 3 of the Institutes, Calvin maintains that God foreknew that the message contained in what Brunner calls the "revelation in creation" would not be understood by sinful men.

39. See Teresa's Life, Ch. 20, para. 33; Ch. 21, para. 10; Ch. 25, para. 5; Ch. 28, para. 19. The last quoted passage is from the Life, Ch. 28, para. 15. See also Poulain, Graces of Interior Prayer, Ch. 22, paras. 16 and 49-50.

40. Ascent, II, Ch. 15, Sec. 2; and Ch. 16, Sec. 10.

41. Ascent, II, Ch. 17, Sec. 6.

42. Ascent, II, Ch. 17, Sec. 4. Italics are mine.

43. Cf. Ascent, II, Ch. 17, Secs. 3 and 4. The term "illumination" is used in the passage quoted above from Ch. 24, Sec. 6.

44. That there are no more articles of the Faith to be revealed is emphasized again by John in Ascent, II, Ch. 22; see esp. Secs. 3, 5 and 7. That an item should be believed because it is revealed to the Church and not because it is revealed in an apprehension is stressed again in Ascent, II, Ch. 21, Sec. 4.

97

45. <u>Ascent</u>, II, Ch. 16, Secs. 10-11; Ch. 17, Secs. 7-9.

46. <u>Ascent</u>, II, Ch. 26, Secs. 11 and 17.

47. I am indebted to a host of people who have read and commented on earlier versions of this paper. Those to whom I am especially grateful include David White (St. John Fisher College), Paul Draper (University of California, Irvine), M. Pabst Battin (University of Utah) and Steven Payne, D. O. (Discalced Carmelite Friars, Washington, D. C.). Also, I should here like to express my gratitude to the philosophy majors at Fullerton whose thoughtful comments on this paper contributed greatly to the discussion at the 11th Annual California State Fullerton Philosophy Conference in 1979.

Towards a Philosophy of
Religious Pluralism
John Hick

From the point of view of phenomenology, or description, the
fact of religious pluralism presents no philosophical problem. It
just is the case that there are many different traditions of
religious life and thought. Their histories, and their
interactions with one another and with other aspects of the human
story, have been traced in increasing detail during the last
hundred and fifty years or so; and indeed knowledge of the
religious life of mankind has now multiplied to the point at which
it far exceeds the receptivity of any one mind. There is
available to us a fascinating plethora of information concerning
religious practices and beliefs, worship and ethics, creeds and
theologies, myths, poetry, music and architecture, reported
religious and mystical experiences, and the interactions of all
these with one another. But simply as historical fact none of
this raises a problem of religious pluralism. It is only when we
add what can be called the basic religious conviction that a
problem is generated.

By the basic religious conviction I mean the conviction that
the realm of religious experience and belief is our human response
to a transcendent divine reality or realities. It is the
conviction, in other words, that religion is not, as a totality,
illusion and self-deception. Whether this conviction is
justified, and if so how that justification is to be spelled out,
is the central issue in the philosophy of religion; and on other
occasions I have, together with many others, addressed myself to
that issue. But on this occasion I propose to consider a further
problem which arises if one adopts that basic religious
conviction. One may actually share that conviction (as I do), or
one may simply be interested to see what the implications of
religious pluralism are for religious belief. But on whichever
basis let us, for the purposes of the present discussion, assume
hypothetically the truth of the basic religious conviction and ask
ourselves how the facts of religious pluralism may then be
understood.

The basic religious conviction normally takes the form of the
claim that some one particular religion is a valid response to the
divine, a response embodying true beliefs concerning the nature of
reality. And the problem of religious pluralism arises from the
fact that there are many such claims. In view of this variety of
gospels it would seem on the face of it that they cannot all be
true; and in that case may they not very well all be false? This
is the problem that is generated by the fact of religious
pluralism in conjunction with the basic religious conviction.

However in adopting the basic religious conviction we are not obliged to assume that all religious experience is straightforwardly veridical or all religious belief straightforwardly true. On the contrary our human nature and circumstances may well make their own contribution to our religious awareness, a contribution in which the range of individual and social mentalities and of cultural forms produces a corresponding variety of perceptions, or it may be of partial distortions, in our human consciousness of the divine. But we are nevertheless assuming that, basically, religion is a range of responses to reality - even if variously inadequate responses - rather than being pure projection or illusion.

Clearly this assumption must, unless good reasons to the contrary are produced, be applied to the entire realm of religions and not only to one favoured religion. I cannot then, as a Christian, solve the problem of religious pluralism by holding that my own religion is a response to the divine reality but that the others are merely human projections. I cannot say, with Karl Barth, that "the Christian religion is true, because it has pleased God, who alone can be the judge in this matter, to affirm it to be the true religion," so that "it alone has the commission and the authority to be a missionary religion, i.e. to confront the world of religions as the one true religion, with absolute self-confidence to invite and challenge it to abandon its ways and to start on the Christian way" (Church Dogmatics, I/2, pp. 350 & 357). Such sublime bigotry could only be possible for one who had no real interest in or awareness of the wider religious life of mankind. For it is evident, when one witnesses worship within the great world faiths, including Christianity, that the same sort of thing is going on in each, namely the directing of the worshippers' attention upon a (putative) higher and transcendent reality, in relation to which lies the human being's ultimate good. There may be clear and convincing criteria by which some forms of religion can be seen to be 'better' or 'higher' than others. But if we restrict our attention to the great world traditions the only criterion by which any of these could be judged to be the one and only true religion, with all the others dismissed as false, would be its own dogmatic assertion, in its more chauvinistic moments, to this effect.

Let us then look at the religious scene and consider how its pluralism is to be understood.

At the outset we encounter a terminological problem to which there seems to be no satisfactory solution. How are we to name the postulated transcendent reality to which we are assuming that religion is man's response? One is initially inclined to reject the word 'God' as too theistic - for the religious spectrum includes major non-theistic as well as theistic traditions - and to consider such alternatives as 'the Transcendent', 'the Divine', 'the Dharma', 'the Absolute', 'the Tao', 'Being itself','Brahman', 'the ultimate divine Reality'. The fact is however that we have no fully tradition-neutral or tradition-transcending term. One is therefore obliged to use a term provided by a particular tradition, but to use it (or consciously to misuse it) in a way which moves beyond the bounds of that tradition. As a Christian I shall accordingly use the word 'God', but shall not use it in a straightforwardly theistic sense. There is of course a danger that either the writer or the reader may slip back without noticing it into the standard use of the term; and both must try to be vigilant against this. I shall then, in what follows, speak of God, but with the important proviso that it is an open question at this stage whether, and if so in what sense, God is personal. We shall in fact, I believe, be led to distinguish between God, and God as conceived and experienced by human beings. God is neither a person nor a thing, but is the transcendent reality which is conceived and experienced by different human mentalities in both personal and non-personal ways.

The general conception of a distinction between, on the one hand, the Godhead in its own infinite depths beyond human experience and comprehension and, on the other hand, the Godhead as finitely experienced by humanity, is both ancient and widespread. Perhaps its most explicit form is the Hindu distinction between nirguna Brahman, Brahman without attributes, beyond the scope of human language, and saguna Brahman, Brahman with attributes, known within human religious experience as Ishvara, the personal creator and governor of the universe. In the West the Christian mystic Meister Eckhart distinguished between the Godhead (Deitas) and God (Deus); and Rudolf Otto in his comparative study of Eckhart and Shankara says, "Herein lies the most extraordinary analogy between Eckhart and Sankara: high above God and the personal Lord abides the 'Godhead', having an almost identical relationship to God as that of Brahman to Isvara" (Mysticism East and West, New York: Meridian Books, p. 14). The Taoist scripture, the Tao Te Ching, begins by affirming that "The Tao that can be expressed is not the eternal Tao." The Jewish Kabbalist mystics distinguished between En Soph, the absolute divine reality beyond human description, and the God of the Bible; and among the Sufis, Al Haqq, the Real, seems to be a similar concept, as the abyss of Godhead underlying the personal Allah. More recently Paul Tillich has spoken of "the God above the God of theism" (The Courage to Be, p. 190) and has said that "God is the symbol of God" (Dynamics of Faith, p. 46). Whitehead, and the process theologians who have followed him, distinguish between the primordial and consequent natures of God, the former being his nature in himself, and the latter being constituted by his inclusion of and response to the world. And Gordon Kaufman has recently distinguished between the "real God" and the "available God," the former being an "utterly unknowable X" and the latter "essentially a mental or imaginative construction" (God the Problem, p. 86). A traditional Christian form of the distinction is that between God in himself, in his infinite self-existent being, beyond the grasp of the human mind, and God in relation to mankind, revealed as creator and redeemer. In one form or another such a distinction seems unavoidable for any view which is not willing to reduce God to a finite being, wholly knowable by the human mind and definable in human concepts. The infinite God must pass out into sheer mystery beyond the reach of our knowledge and comprehension, and is in this limitless transcendence nirguna, the ultimate Godhead, the God above the God of theism.

There are in fact, I would suggest, three main types of religious experience. The most common is the experience of God as a personal presence and will, known in I-Thou encounter. This experience is the heart of theistic religion, in the Eastern as well as in the Western traditions. The second type is the nature - or cosmic - mysticism in which the whole world or the whole universe is experienced as the manifestation or vehicle of divine reality - as in Wordsworth's famous lines:

> And I have felt
> A presence that disturbs me with the joy
> Of something far more deeply interfused
> Whose dwelling is the light of setting suns,
> And the round ocean and the living air,
> And the blue sky, and in the mind of man:
> A motion and a spirit, that impels
> All thinking things, all objects of all thought,
> And rolls through all things.

In such experiences God is not known as personal, nor yet as impersonal, but rather as more than personal - as living, as the ultimate source of value, and yet as altogether transcending the notion of an encountered person, on however tremendous a scale. And the third type is that in which the experiencing self is temporarily absorbed into the divine reality, becoming one with the One. Since personality is essentially interpersonal, so that one is a person only in relationship with other persons, there is no personal existence or encounter within this unitive moment. This is perhaps the mystical state par excellence, apparently experienced by some, but described by none; for it is beyond the scope of human language.

Now these are all finite experiences of finite creatures. (This is true even of the unitive experience; for the experiencer returns from it, still a finite individual, to try to speak of what has happened to him.) If we assume, with the major religious traditions, that God is infinite, then we have to say that these forms of religious experience are not experiences of the infinitude of God - which no finite experience could ever encompass - but of God as finitely experienced by particular human consciousnesses. And in understanding such a plurality of experiences we have to take account of the contribution of the human mind itself to all our awareness of our environment, divine as well as natural. I shall be arguing that these different forms of religious awareness are not necessarily competitive, in the sense that the validity of one entails the spuriousness of the others, but are better understood as different phenomenal experiences of the one divine noumenon; or in another language, different experiential transformations of the same transcendent informational input.

I shall return in due course to the non-personal forms of religious awareness; but let us first approach the idea of a divine phenomenon through the theistic type of religious experience.

If one were to list all the many gods whose names we know from the literature and traditions of India (such as Rudra, Agni, Mitra, Indra, Varuna...) and of the Near East (such as Osiris, Isis, Horus, Ra, Jahweh...) and of southern Europe (such as Jupiter, Apollo, Dionysus, Poseidon...) and of northern Europe (such as Odin, Thor, Balder, Vali, Woden...) and of Africa (such as Nabongo, Luhanga, Nyame, Lesa, Ruhanga...) and also of the Americas, Australasia, Northern Asia and the rest of the world, they would probably form a list as long as the telephone directory of a large city. What are we to say about all these gods? Do we say that they all exist? And what would it be for a named god, say Balder, with his distinctive characteristics, to exist? In any straightforward sense it would, I suggest, at least involve there being a consciousness, answering to this name, in addition to all the millions of human consciousnesses. Are we then to say that for each name in our directory of gods there is an additional consciousness enjoying the further set of attributes specified by the concept of that particular god? In most cases this would be theoretically possible since in most cases the gods are explicitly or implicitly finite beings whose powers and spheres of operation are at least approximately known; and many of them could co-exist without contradiction. On the other hand, the gods of the monotheistic faiths are thought of in each case as the one and only God, so that it is impossible for more than one of them to instantiate this concept. It does not seem, then, that we can possibly say that all the named gods, and particularly not all the most important ones, exist, at any rate not in any simple and straightforward sense. Nor, having assumed the basic religious conviction of the reality of the divine, can we say in any straightforward sense that they are all non-existent and man's whole supposed awareness of divine beings and powers illusory. Nor, again, as I have already indicated, can we take refuge in the claim that the God of one's own religion is real and all the others either illusory or, perhaps, non-divine demonic beings. Instead let us explore the possibility that the immediate object of theistic religious awareness is what I shall call an 'image' of God; and that the plurality of such images arises from the various ways in which the divine reality has impinged upon the human consciousness in its different circumstances.

But first we must establish the distinction between God and our human images of God. Within the Judaic-Christian tradition we see the need for such a distinction when we ask ourselves whether God is really male, as distinguished from female, or whether on the contrary God transcends the distinction between men and women but has commonly been thought of as male within patriarchal societies. I believe that most of us today will give the latter answer. Although in the Bible God is consistently referred to as 'He' and is described, metaphorically, as king, father, warrior, shepherd, etc., yet surely God is not in fact a larger or even an infinite man as distinguished from woman, but can be thought of equally appropriately in male and female terms. In this respect much Indian devotional language, in which God is addressed as mother as well as father, is to be preferred to the exclusively masculine language of the semitic faiths. But the point at the moment is that if God is not in reality male as distinguished from female, but is nevertheless imaged as such in many religious traditions, then we are obliged to draw a distinction between God and our human images of God - in this case between God and our distinctively masculine images of God.

But what, more precisely, do we mean by an 'image' of God? We can I think find partial analogies in the varied impressions of the same individual in the minds of different historians. Consider a personage, X, who lived in the past and who is therefore not directly accessible to us, about whom certain salient facts are known but such that any concrete impression of X's character leaves a good deal to the constructive imagination of the historian. Any such impression or, as I shall call it, image, represents an interpretation of the available data. Varying images of X may form in the minds of writers in different subsequent periods, with their different cultural backgrounds; and there may be both popular, often oversimplified, images and caricatures as well as more academic images. There are a number of famous historical figures to whom all this applies - for example, Mary Queen of Scots, King Charles I, Napoleon, Abraham Lincoln, Mahatma Gandhi, Stalin, Chairman Mao ... In such cases the distinction seems inevitable between the historical individual *an sich* and the images in terms of which he or she has become known to later consciousness. This is of course only a partial analogy; I am not suggesting that God existed in the past but does not exist today. The analogy is rather with the varying images in terms of which we may be aware of an historical figure. An image of this kind represents data moulded into concrete forms by the imagination in accordance with the selective attention of the historian. And the more a figure engages our interest by touching our own vital concerns - a concern, for example, for justice or freedom - the greater tends to be the subjective contribution to our image of him or her. And when we turn to those who are religiously significant to us, and who accordingly help to form the basic orientation of our lives, the subjective contribution generally increases yet further in importance. Because a saint, or messiah, or avatar, or bodhissatva, or arahant, or spiritual master or guru meets some spiritual need in us, and so has salvific power in our lives, our image of such a person naturally emphasises holiness, goodness, wisdom and remarkable powers; and further the image tends to expand as the tradition in which it is embedded develops. These images of saints - and I am referring to personality-impressions of them rather than to physical representations - extend the analogy in the direction of our images of God. Within Christianity, catholic spirituality is particularly rich in examples. The faithful often address an individual saint, or Mary, Mother of Jesus, asking him or her to perform some miracle or to intercede for them with God the Father. In the case of Mary distinctive local versions are cherished within particular communities. Thus there is Our Lady of Lourdes, who appeared as a young girl eighteen times to Bernadette Soubirous in 1858, speaking to her on several occasions, thereby founding a place of pilgrimage and healing to which many thousands go each year. Or Our Lady of Fatima, in Portugal, who made prophecies about when the first world war was to end, about developments in Russia, and about another war in the future. And there is our Lady of Walsingham, and other local miraculous versions of Mary in many countries. Thus if we assume that the Virgin Mary is an existing personal being, now exalted into heaven but still actively concerned with the affairs of living men and women, we are led to distinguish between Mary herself and a variety of partially different human images of her. It does not however necessarily follow from the fact of their plurality that these images are false. The alternative possibility is that they arise from genuine encounters with Mary in which, as she has met the varying needs of different individuals and communities, different images of her have legitimately been formed.

An even closer analogy to our images of God is provided, within Christianity, by the different images of Christ. For the historical Jesus is a prime example of someone who has given rise to a range of images expressing a variety of interpretive responses. He has for example been perceived, or imaged, or responded to as God incarnate; as a human teacher of the fatherhood of God and the brotherhood of man; as an apocalyptic preacher of the imminent end of history; as 'gentle Jesus meek and mild'; as a social radical proclaiming that the lowly are to be exalted and the mighty brought down; as the 'man for others', the embodiment of self-giving love; and of course as various mixtures of these. Different popular images of Jesus are expressed in the growing number of interpretations of him in films and rock operas. Merely to list these different Jesuses of the religious and secular imagination is to recognize a distinction between the historical individual who lived in Galilee nineteen centuries ago, concerning whom we have rather few items of secure information, and the plurality of images of him operating in the minds of different individuals and groups and communal traditions. But beyond this, the historical Jesus has expanded in Christian thought and experience into two further Christ figures who are distinct (in that they have been able to operate within different streams of spirituality) and yet also capable of merging into one (in yet other forms of spirituality). One of these is the cosmic

Christ, the eternal divine Son, 'seated at the right hand of the Father' as the second person of the Holy Trinity. This cosmic Christ has been imaged in very different ways in different periods of history and in different branches of the Church - as the imperial Pantocrator, as Victor over the Devil, as the terrible Judge before whom his Mother had to intercede for human sinners, and often in the modern Church as the spirit of divine love. But given this plurality of images there remains the possibility that they represent different and partial human awarenesses of the same transcendent cosmic being. The other Christ-figure is the personal Jesus-presence reported by many Christians as a living being to whom they speak and who in some manner speaks to them and sometimes directs their lives. This presence may be known at any one time to a number of different Christians in different places, being experienced in varying ways related to their personal situations and needs. The object of each believer's consciousness, in these cases, is his or her own image of Jesus; and the question which again remains open is whether these images are simply projections of the imagination or are joint creations of human imagination and an informing input from the living person of Jesus. It seems clear that to some extent Christians each have their own images of the risen lord; but it remains possible that the risen Jesus is meeting them and interacting with them, in ways related to their own spiritual needs and capacities, through these different images of him. But whatever ontological status we attribute to the different versions of the Jesus-presence and of the cosmic Christ, we are obliged to recognise a distinction between this plurality of images and the person whose images they are.

A further analogy, which may be illuminating to some even though possibly not to others, comes from parapsychology. One of the types of phenomena studied is that in which a medium goes into a trance and it seems that the still living consciousness of someone who has physically died - let us call him John Smith - communicates though the medium's vocal machinery. Sometimes the 'spirit' speaks in a way which is recognisably that of the John Smith whom he claims to be, and sometimes also his conversation includes items of information which could hardly have been known to the medium. To account for all this the theory has been advanced that the conscious, speaking, responding personality who is controlling the medium's vocal apparatus is a secondary personality, a fragment of the medium's mind which takes over in the trance state. This secondary personality plays roles suggested to it and indeed often puts considerable intelligence and skill into its productions - somewhat as in the case of hypnotised persons who may play on command the role of, say, guests at a banquet or of visitors from outer space. In the spiritualist seance it may be that the informational input which informs the performance is derived telepathically from the sitters. But the further possibility has been suggested that some of the input may come from the deceased individual John Smith, who is being impersonated by the medium's secondary personality. In that case John Smith is, in this doubtless frustratingly indirect and unreliable way, communicating with his friends on earth. If this is so, the sitters are in contact with a dramatic personation of John Smith, produced by a secondary personality of the medium, but based at least partly on information deriving from John Smith himself. Thus it is possible that he communicates at different times to different groups of sitters through varying dramatic images of himself formed in the minds of different mediums. Here again we are led to a distinction between John Smith an sich and a plurality of, in this case, speaking and responding images of him which are partly similar and partly different.

I do not want to pursue here the possible functional analogy between spiritualist mediums and the prophets, avatars, gurus, etc., through whom God is believed to speak to mankind. I want instead to develop a different aspect of the theory of mediumship to which I have referred. In doing so it will be helpful to use the notion of information, not in the familiar propositional sense of 'items of information' but in the modern cybernetic sense of cognitive input which can be expressed in different modes and which can be transformed from one mode to another. The value of this concept lies precisely in its generality. Whatever influences or impacts from our surrounding world affect one's state as a self-directing part of that world constitute information: in the definition of Norbert Wiener, the father of Cybernetics, "Information is a name for the content of what is exchanged with the outer world as we adjust to it, and make our adjustment felt upon it" (The Human Use of Human Beings, London: Sphere Books, 1968, p. 19). Thus information passes in the form of light waves from a lighted object to the retina of the eye, is there transformed into chemical changes in the rods and cones, and then into electrical impulses passing up the strands of the optic nerve into the brain, and finally into the conscious experience of seeing the object which had been reflecting light into our eye. Or again, information flows along the wire from the aerial into the television set and is there transformed into a picture on the screen; or along the telephone wire to be transformed into the sound of a voice. In such cases the same information is being expressed in a variety of ways. And whenever there is transformation from one coding to another there is the possibility of distortion of the information. Indeed there is a general tendency for information to deteriorate as it functions. The picture on the TV screen may be distorted or blurred; and the machinery of the brain can likewise be damaged and produce a distorted version of the environment in consciousness. There are mechanical failures, comparable with the errors to which an electronic calculator is liable when its battery is insufficiently charged. But in addition to the mechanical transformation of information studied by cybernetics there is also, and more importantly, its interpretation by the mind into units or moments of meaning. For at the distinctively human level of consciousness

we inhabit a more or less familiar and ordered world with
recognisable characteristics to which we know how to respond.
(There is of course also novelty and surprise, but always within
the context of a familiar basic framework.) All our consciousness
of objects and of situations is an experience of them as having a
certain character such that it is appropriate to behave in
relation to them, or within them, in this rather than in that way.
Such awareness represents a fusion between, on the one hand, the
information reaching us from our environment and, on the other
hand, the system of concepts in terms of which that information
comes to consciousness as organised and meaningful experience. In
this procedure - which constitutes normal perception - the
function of our system of concepts, or recognitional capacities,
is to guide the pre-conscious interpretive process whereby sensory
information is transformed into our actual consciousness of the
world. The word 'meaning' is appropriate as pointing to the way
in which our awareness of our environment, as having the character
that we experience it to have, is related to our own practical
responses to it. To say that the perceived world has meaning to
us is to say that it is a world which we can inhabit by acting and
reacting in accordance with its perceived character. For meaning,
in this sense, is meaning for someone; it is the difference which
awareness of the presence of this particular thing, or of being in
this particular environing situation, makes to the perceiver's
dispositional stance. Thus, to be conscious that the object which
I am now holding in my hand is a pen is to be in a distinctive
dispositional state in relation to it, such that I expect it to
make marks in ink but not to bite or talk, and such that I shall
use it for writing but not normally for any other purpose. And in
general our awareness of our environment as having the complex
character that we perceive it to have consists in part in our
being in a correspondingly complex dispositional state in relation
to it.

This general account of cognition also applies to our
awareness (whether veridical or illusory) of the religious
meaning, of character, of situations. For our human commerce with
God does not consist only or even mainly in our holding certain
beliefs, but above all in experiencing the reality of God as the
lord in whose presence one is, and in experiencing the power of
God in the events of one's own life and of the wider history with
which this is continuous. When for example Jeremiah perceived the
Babylonian army, marching on Jerusalem, as God's agent to punish
his unfaithful people, he was interpreting the events of his time
in terms of his image of God, this interpretation coming to
consciousness in his awareness of God as actively at work in the
events of the world around him, and having its dispositional
correlate in his inner compulsion to proclaim the religious
meaning of these events. Or when today a theistic believer has
some degree of awarness of existing in the unseen presence of God,
he is interpreting his total situation in religious terms. This
interpretation comes to consciousness as the experience that in

and through all his dealings with the world and with other people he is also having to do with the transcendent God; and this awareness is embodied in his dispositional state in, for example, tendencies to engage in acts of worship, to think and feel in certain ways and to behave in accordance with associated ethical norms.

What part, then, is played in this religious awareness by images of God? Essentially the part, I suggest, that is played in sense perception by the concepts or recognitional capacities in terms of which we are conscious of the objects and situations constituting our physical environment.

It was above all Immanuel Kant, with his doctrine that we are necessarily aware of the world in terms of certain forms and categories inherent in the structure of a unitary finite consciousness, who has enabled the modern world to recognise the mind's own positive contribution to the meaningful character of its perceived environment. The view that I am proposing is in some respects Kantian and in other respects un-Kantian, and it may perhaps be useful at this point to bring out the analogies and disanalogies with the Kantian model. Kant is himself notoriously difficult to interpret, largely because the Critique of Pure Reason contains several different strands of argument whose mutual consistency can be questioned and whose relative importance can be variously estimated. The strand that I shall be using is the distinction between phenomenon and noumenon, but transposed from the problem of sense perception to that of the awareness of God. In using something analogous to Kant's phenomenon/noumenon distinction I am not opting for any view of the place of this distinction in the Critique. I am in fact not concerned at all with questions of Kantian interpretation or of the general assessment of Kant's critical philosophy. I am, rather, taking a structural model from his system and using it in a sphere - the epistemology of religion - which Kant treated in a very different way, and in relation to a problem within that sphere which had hardly begun to be recognised in his time. It should also be stressed that Kant himself would not have sanctioned the idea that we in any way experience God, even as divine phenomenon in distinction from divine noumenon. God was not for him a reality encountered in religious experience, but an object postulated by reason on the basis of its own practical functioning as moral agent. The reality of moral obligation presupposes the reality of God as the basis of the possibility of the summum bonum in which perfect goodness and perfect happiness coincide. God must accordingly be postulated as "a cause of the whole of nature, itself distinct from nature, which contains the ground of the exact coincidence of happiness with morality" (Critique of Practical Reason, Book II, Chap. V, p. 125). The idea of God, thus indirectly established, also functions as a regulative idea whereby we "regard all order in the world as if it had originated in the purpose of a supreme reason" (Critique of Pure Reason, Appendix to the Transcendental Dialectic, p. B 714). Thus for Kant

God is not experienced, but postulated. However I am exploring here the different and very non-Kantian hypothesis that God is experienced by human beings, but experienced in a manner analogous to that in which, according to Kant, we experience the world - namely by informational input from external reality being interpreted by the mind in terms of its own categorial system and thus coming to consciousness as meaningful phenomenal experience. For Kant distinguished - in one strand of his thought - between the noumenal world, which exists independently of and outside man's perception of it, and the phenomenal world, which is that world as it appears to our human consciousness. All that we are entitled to say about the noumenal world is that it is the unknown reality whose informational input produces, in collaboration with the human mind, the phenomenal world of our experience. This happens through the medium of certain concepts which Kant calls the categories of the understanding. In Kant's system the pure categories, or pure concepts of the Understanding (for example, substance), are schematised in terms of temporality to produce the more concrete categories which are exhibited in our actual experience of the world. (For example, the pure concept of substances is schematised as the concept of an object enduring through time.) Something analogous to this, I am suggesting, takes place in our awareness of God. For the religious person experiences the divine, not as a general idea, but under some specific and relatively concrete divine image. An abstract concept of deity, such as the concept of 'the uncreated creator of the universe,' is schematised or concretised in a range of divine images. And if we ask what functions in a role analogous to that of time in the schematisation of the Kantian categories, the answer, I suggest, is the continuum of historical factors which have produced our different religious cultures. It is the variations of the human cultural situation that concretise the notion of deity as specific images of God. And it is these images that inform man's actual religious experience, so that it is an experience specifically of the God of Israel, or of Allah, or of the Father of our Lord Jesus Christ, or of Vishnu or Shiva...

It is desirable to avoid a possible misunderstanding which offers itself at this point. If the worshipper's thought of God only describes an image of God, and the worshipper's experience of God is only the experience of God as thus imaged, does it not follow that worship is directed to an illusion, a mere phenomenal appearance? The answer must echo Kant's statement that his distinction between phenomenon, or appearance, and noumenon, or reality, results in a 'transcendental idealism' which is at the same time an 'empirical realism' (Critique of Pure Reason, p. A 370-2). That is to say, the world as we perceive it is real, not illusory; but it is the appearance to us of that which exists in itself outside our experience of it. The perceptually organized world of colours, sounds and scents, of heat and cold, of solid tables and chairs and trees and animals is entirely real. And yet as humanly perceived it exists only for human perceivers. Animals with different sensory equipment and different forms of consciousness must perceive the world very differently. We are real beings in a real environment; but we experience that environment selectively, in terms of our special cognitive equipment. Something essentially similar has to be said about the human awareness of God. God as experienced by this or that individual or group is real, not illusory; and yet the experience of God is partial and is adapted to our human spiritual capacities. God as humanly known is not God an sich but God in relation to mankind, thought and experienced in terms of some particular limited tradition of religious awareness and response. Thus in expounding this situation we have to try to keep two themes in balance: the agnostic theme that we only know God partially and imperfectly, and the positive theme that we really do know God as practically and savingly related to ourselves.

Let us now apply this thesis to what is perhaps the largest and most obvious contrast between different human awarenesses of the divine, namely as personal and as non-personal.

A number of Christian theologians have distinguished between 'being a person' and 'being personal,' the theological point of the distinction lying in their assumption that whereas a person is necessarily finite a personal being may be infinite. However the distinction is entirely stipulative and has no further use than to avoid the problems connected with the concept of an infinite person. To be personal, surely, is to be a person: the notion of a personal being who is not a person has no content. Accordingly the idea of an infinte personal being is the same as the idea of an infinite person. It is not easy to determine whether this idea is viable, and I do not want to argue the question here. Instead I propose to take account of the modern insight that personality is essentially interpersonal. The medieval concept of a person was that of "an individual rational substance" (Boethius). On this definition it is conceivable for there to be only one person in existence; a person does not inherently need there to be other persons in relation to whom one is oneself a person. On this view we can conceive of God, 'prior to' and independently of his creation, as the eternal and infinite person. But this notion collapses if we adopt the modern understanding of personality as a function of community. On this view, to be a person is to exist in personal interaction with other persons; and the idea of a person existing a se, as the only person in existence, is a self-contradiction. Clearly, this understanding of personality makes it impossible to think of God as eternally personal in his own self-existent being, 'prior' and without relation to his creation.

But cannot this particular problem be met by invoking the Christian conception that God is three persons in one? This doctrine has taken a variety of forms within the long Christian tradition, ranging from the virtual tritheism of the 'social' conceptions of the Trinity to the modalistic notion of three modes of operation of the one God. The latter, whilst in many ways attractive, does not enable us to speak of interpersonal relationships between the hypostases of the Trinity, or thus to speak of the Godhead as inherently and eternally personal. A society of three, sustaining personal relationships between its members, requires three centres of personal consciousness and will, however harmoniously related. Such virtual tritheism is found not only in popular understandings and artistic representations of the Trinity, but also within patristic thought, particularly among the Cappadocian fathers of the fourth century. Thus Gregory of Nazianzus used the example of Adam, Eve and their son Seth, who were three and yet shared the same human nature, as an analogy for the Father, Son and Spirit, who are three whilst sharing the same divine nature. This kind of Trinitarianism does enable us to think of the Godhead, in its eternal nature independently of the creation, as containing personality; for on this interpretation the Godhead consists of three interrelated personal beings forming together an uniquely intimate divine society. But it cannot be concealed that this is a sophisticated form of tritheism. Such a limited polytheism would enable us to think of the Godhead as a community of persons, but would not have solved our original problem of how to think of the God of monotheism as eternally personal.

We cannot, then, meaningfully attribute personality to the infinite and eternal existence of God a se. But on the other hand God is the ground, or creator, or source of personal life, and is in that sense 'more' rather than 'less' than a person. Further God is experienced by finite persons as (though not only as) the divine Thou existing over against them in I-Thou relationship. God is personal, then, in the sense that man's awareness of God as Person is a genuine encounter with the transcendent ground of all existence, including personal existence. Using another language, God experienced as personal is a valid transformation in human consciousness of informational input from the transcendent divine source. But we have to add the significant fact that God has been and is experienced by human beings not only as a person but as a number of different persons, each constituted by God's impingement upon a different human community with its own divine image formed through a particular strand of history. Thus the God of Israel is a specific personal deity with his own historial biography. His personal life - that is, his interactions with a group of finite persons - began with his self-revelation to Abraham and has continued in Jewish religious experience down to the present day. As such he has a distinctive personality, developed in interaction with his chosen people; he is a part of their history and they are part of his. And he is a recognisably different personality from, say, the Lord Krishna, because Krishna exists in relation to a different community, forming and formed by a different culture, and creating and created by a different history. Again, the God who speaks to mankind in the Qur'an is part of yet another history of divine-human relationship...I suggest that this pluralistic situation is rendered intelligible by the hypothesis of one infinite divine noumenon experienced in varying ways within different strands of human history, thereby giving rise to different divine personalities who are each formed in their interactions with a particular community or tradition.

But God is also non-personal. We have to affirm this both in the negative sense that personality is a function of personal interaction and therefore cannot be attributed to the eternal divine nature a se; and in the positive sense that God is validly experienced in non-personal as well as in personal ways. The varying divine personalities worshipped in their respective religious traditions, and likewise the varying non-personal forms in which God is known in yet other religious traditions, are all alike divine phenomena formed by the impact of God upon the plurality of human consciousnesses. I have concentrated here upon the awareness of God as personal; but the other aspect, which I must reserve for later treatment, is equally important.

It will be evident that the above is a significantly different hypothesis from one with which it nevertheless has a partial resemblance, namely the Hindu advaitist view that God, or Brahman, is non-personal, being known as such in the state of full enlightenment, and that the worship of personal Gods belongs to a lower and preliminary stage of the religious life which is eventually to be left behind. In distinction from this I am suggesting that God is to be thought of as the divine noumenon, experienced by mankind as a range of divine phenomena which take both theistic and non-theistic forms.

At first sight the distinction between divine noumenon and divine phenomena might seem to preclude any 'doctrine of God,' or account of the divine nature. For if we only know God as experienced by mankind, and if God is so experienced in a number of different ways, does not the noumenal or real God remain impenetrably hidden from us? Thus Feuerbach attacked the distinction between "God as he is in himself and God as he is for me" as a sceptical distinction (The Essence of Christianity, New York: Harper Torchbook edition, p. 17). And it is true that, on this view, we have to accept that the infinite divine reality is only knowable by man in so far as it impinges upon finite human consciousnesses, with their variously limited and conditioned capacities for awareness and response. But once we accept this, then the very plurality and variety of the human experiences of God provide a wider basis for theology than can the experience of any one religious tradition taken by itself. For whereas we can learn from one tradition that God is personal, as the noumenal ground of theistic experience, and from another tradition that God is the non-personal Void, as the noumenal ground of its form of mystical experience, we learn from the two together that God is the ground and source of both types of experience and is in that sense both personal and non-personal.

If we now ask, from within the basic religious conviction, why God should be known in such variously imperfect ways, the answer must, I think, hinge upon the fact of finite freedom and the variety of forms which human life has taken in the ramifying exercise of this freedom. We have to consider the difference between, on the one hand, being conscious of the world and of other human beings and, on the other hand, being conscious of God.

We are not diminished in our essential freedom by being aware of the existence of entities below ourselves in the scale of value or of reality. For although the power of storm and earthquake, or the strength of elephant or tiger, dwarfs my own strength, and the vastness of the universe around us reveals us by comparison as microscopically small, yet humanity nevertheless transcends the whole world of nature, with all its immensity and power, by the very fact of consciousness of it; as Pascal said, "if the universe were to crush him, man would still be more noble than that which killed him, because he knows that he dies and the advantage which the universe has over him; the universe knows nothing of this" (Pensees, No. 347). And again in relation to other human beings, whilst many are more intelligent, or more wealthy, or more powerful, etc., yet they are still in the end only fellow mortals, and thus ultimately on the same level as myself. But on the other hand, in relation to that which has absolute reality and value, I am nothing and can have no personal being and freedom in relation to it unless the infinitely valuable reality permits me largely to shut it out of my consciousness. Thus we preserve our freedom over against the infinite reality which, as absolute value, makes a total claim upon us, by being aware of it in terms of limited and limiting concepts and images.

Religious awareness is in this respect continuous with our awareness of other aspects of our environment. For our cognitive machinery, consisting in our sense organs and neuro-system together with the selecting and organising activity of the mind/brain, has a twofold function: to make us aware of certain aspects of our environment and at the same time to preserve us from being aware of other aspects of it. Shutting out is as important as letting in. It begins in our sensory equipment, which is selectively sensitive only to a minute proportion of the total range of information flowing from our physical environment - only a very small fraction, for example, of the full range of light and sound and other waves which are impinging upon us all the time. And it is essential to our survival and well-being that this should be so. If, for example, instead of seeing water as the continuous shiny substance that we drink, we perceived it as a cloud of electrons in rapid swirling motion, and the glass which holds it as a mass of brilliantly coloured crystals, themselves composed of particles in violent activity, we should be bewildered by such an excess of information and should be unable to react appropriately. And so both senses and mind/brain select, and then relate and organise within the framework of well-tried categories and patterns, with the result that we perceive a version of the world which is enormously simplified and yet such that we can inhabit it successfully.

This need to shut out many aspects of reality in order to live as the finite creatures that we are, not only limited but limited in our specifically human ways, also applies, I have been suggesting, to our consciousness of God. We have a system for filtering out the infinite divine reality and reducing it to forms with which we can cope. This system is religion, which is our resistance (in a sense analogous to that used in electronics) to God. The function of the different religions is to enable us to be conscious of God, and yet only partially and selectively, in step with our own spiritual development, both communal and individual.

It is important to remember that religious traditions, considered as 'filters' or 'resistances,' function as totalities which include not only concepts and images of God with the modes of religious experience which they inform, but also systems of doctrine, ritual and myth, and art forms, moral codes, lifestyles and often patterns of social organisation. For religions are communal responses to God, rooted in the life of societies and forming an important, indeed often a dominant, aspect of their culture. Accordingly the spread of religions through missionary activity has usually also been the spread of their associated cultures; and the contemporary phenomenon of individuals being converted from one religion to another whilst remaining within their original culture, so that for example, we have Buddhist, Hindu and Muslim converts within Western societies - is a new and confusing though perhaps creative development.

Let us now look, in the briefest possible way, at the application of this broad interpretive conception to the religious history of mankind. Man is a thoroughly historical creature, living through a changing continuum of contingent circumstances into which he has emerged from a primitive prehistoric condition which itself evolved out of lower forms of life. Thus the human awareness of God must be expected to have undergone development though changing historical circumstances, the cumulative growth of traditions, and the influence of those outstanding individuals, prophets and saints, who have in their own individual freedom been more open to God than the societies of which they were members. The influence of such spiritual and moral leaders is crucial; for we are not looking at a natural process of evolution but at a history with all the complex and sometimes conflicting contingencies generated by human freedom. In the earliest stages of this history God was reduced in human awareness to the dimensions of man's own image, so that the gods were, like human kings, often cruel and bloodthirsty; or to the dimensions of the tribe or nation, as the symbol of its unity and power; or again to the more ample dimensions of the forces of nature, such as the life-giving and yet burning radiance of the sun, or the destructive power of storm and earthquake, or the mysterious pervasive force of fertility, and the response that was required, the way of life which such awareness rendered appropriate, was a communal response. The anthropologists have taught us how closely knit primitive societies have been, and how little scope they offered for individual thought, whether in religion or in other aspects of life. It was only with the gradual emergence of individuality, in what Jaspers has called the axial period, particularly from about 800 B. C., that higher conceptions of God developed, in correlation with a deeper sense of a moral claim upon human life. For it was the emergence of the individual, and in particular of the religious individual, that made possible the outstanding spiritual leaders on whose consciousness God impinged in new ways or with new intensity and power. The greatest of these became the founders of continuing religious traditions - Moses, Zoroaster, Confucius, Gautama, Jesus and later Mohammad. Others effected important developments within existing traditions - the Hebrew prophets; the writers of the Upanishads, of the Tao Te Ching, and of the Gita; Pythagoras, Socrates, Plato, Guru Nanak. These great traditions have continued to develop in larger and smaller ways through the centuries, ramifying out into the vast and complex ideological organisms which we know as the world religions. These religions are thus based upon different human perceptions of, and embody different human responses to, the infinite reality of God.

Let me now end by pointing forward to the next major question that arises if one opts for some such hypothesis as this. I have just referred to the different world religions, with their different images of God. Our question concerns the relative adequacy or value of these different images, both theistic and non-theistic. For it is clearly possible that they are not all equally adequate, but that some mediate God to mankind better than others. Indeed it would be hard to maintain - to take examples from the Judaic-Christian scriptures - that the image of God as a bloodthirsty tribal deity urging the Israelites to slaughter their neighbours (Deuteronomy 7:16), and the image of God conveyed in Jesus' parable of the prodigal son (Luke 15:11-32), are equal in validity or adequacy or value. But by what criteria do we assess such images; and how do we establish such criteria?

We saw early in this paper that it would be unreasonable for any religion to claim to be alone authentic, dismissing all the others as false. But it remains entirely possible that more adequate and less adequate images of God operate within different religious traditions. How are we to evaluate these images? This is the large and difficult question that next arises.

Published in Neue Zeitschrift fur Systematische Theologie und Religionsphilosophie 22. Band 1980 Heft 2. Reprinted by permission of Walter de Gruyter & Co.

Conceptual Relativism and
Religious Experience
Joseph Runzo

Relativism has emerged as a central and powerful element within theology in this century. Theological relativism is part of the larger fabric of the relativist orientation which has become common in such social sciences as archaeology, sociology, ethnology, and psychology, in the work of philosophers of science like Thomas Kuhn, as well as in society at large. But theological relativism is not a mere patchwork of relativistic movements in other disciplines. It has its own lineage of whole cloth, traceable through H. R. Niebuhr and Ernst Troeltsch, Friedrich Schleiermacher and others, back to the skeptical attitude toward absolutist religious authority and dogma which was a legacy of the sixteenth-century Reformation. Moreover, the conditions for theological relativism are latent in the very enterprise of theology. As Paul Tillich points out, "Theology moves back and forth between two poles, the eternal truth of its foundation and the temporal situation in which the eternal truth must be received" (1). Theology is always compelled to address the present. But more recently this concern has been coupled with an acute historicist sense of past and present differences among the enculturated patterns of human thought to which - and out of which - theology must speak. Thus H. R. Niebuhr remarks, "in every work of culture, we relative men, with our relative points of view and relative evaluations, deal with relative values..." (2).

As a result some form of conceptual relativism has often been accepted in modern theology. In general, conceptual relativism is the view that what is true depends on a society's conceptual schema(s) - that is, depends on those cognitive resources, principally concepts, beliefs, and their interrelationships, which the members of any given society bring to experience, thereby ordering their "world." Rephrased then, conceptual relativism is the epistemological position that the truth of statements (3) is relative to the conceptual schema(s) from within which they are formulated and/or assessed. Expressed in theology as theological relativism, this is the view that what is religious truth within one period of church history, or within one religious society, is false or merely mythological within another period or society, and vice versa.

This view is usually derived from the historicist recognition that, e.g., the thought worlds of the first-century church and of the twentieth-century church, like that of many Christians and that of many Buddhists, are, at least in part if not wholly, incommensurate. Yet on a conceptual relativist view about

117

religious belief, each body of religious beliefs, though incompatible with contrasting bodies of religious belief, can be in itself a proper view of reality. For it is an important consequence of a conceptual relativist view that there is a distinct conception or set of conceptions of reality, corresponding to each conceptual schema. Thus in a certain sense, those possessing one conceptual schema live in a different world - i.e., reality is different for them - than those possessing a different conceptual schema. And on this position it would be improper to employ one such conceptual-schema-relative notion of reality, in order to criticize the view of reality expressed or expressible within another schema, as simply being false. Applied to religion, this would mean that each set of religious beliefs is to be judged internally according to its own internally consistent standards. (It need not follow that different sets of religious beliefs are utterly mutually exclusive. Incompatible sets of religious beliefs might still share certain portions of their respective propositional content as a common element.)

I think that a conceptual relativist epistemology of the sort I have just described is, in general, intelligible, and I think that some version of conceptual relativism can be defended (though I will not attempt such a defense in this paper) (5). But even allowing that the general epistemological position of conceptual relativism is intelligible, and further defensible, when a theist, and particularly when a theologian, accedes to conceptual relativism, a particularly acute and important issue arises: If conceptual relativism is accepted, does this allow for any possible way of avoiding enculturated, relative conceptions, so that one could achieve an absolute understanding of or insight into the nature and acts of God? This issue arises for theological relativism because it seems to be part of the very point of doing theology to attempt to provide a better understanding of the truth about God and His acts - what Tillich refers to as "the eternal truth" which is the foundation of theology. And this issue is acute because the acceptance of some form of conceptual relativism appears prima facie inconsistent with the project of achieving a better understanding of the reality denoted by "God," a reality presumed to be self-subsistent and objectively real.

Now it certainly seems as if there should be some possible means of evading the relativizing effects of our conceptual schemas and achieving an absolute insight into the nature and acts of God. And the obvious candidate which presents itself is religious experience. Would not experiences of God, if veridical, provide precisely the sort of direct and absolute insight needed?

Friedrich Schleiermacher, the great nineteenth-century theologian, gave seminal expression both to the issue of relativism vs. absolutism in theology, and to this type of appeal to religious experience. Regarding relativism, Schleiermacher holds that while true religion concerns absolutes, particular religions are "a product of time and history"(4): they are human

118

institutions, subject to the vicissitudes of cultural context and changes of human perspective over time. Within this dichotomy, theology, while attempting an absolute view of God, is firmly embedded in the category of enculturated human construction, and hence of relativism. And regarding a solution to this difficulty, Schleiermacher suggests that religious experience itself provides an understanding of the divine which is unaffected by relativism. In particular, he thinks that an "immediate consciousness of the Deity" - that is, a pure experience which does not involve conceptualizations, and an immediate experience that does not involve any mind-dependent inferences - will circumvent the relativity of our human conceptions.

The question I will address in this paper, then, is this: in the face of conceptual relativism, can such an appeal to religious experience solve the relativist-absolutist tension in theology which Schleiermacher exposes? I will first assess Schleiermacher's own analysis and utilization of religious experience. I will then turn to the more recent attempts of Martin Buber to base true piety on direct religious experience. After arguing that both these attempts fail, I will analyze the more extreme claim, which is sometimes made about the Christian mystical tradition, that special, profound mystical experiences can provide an absolute understanding of God. Regarding mysticism proper, I will first consider the epistemic status of mystical visions, and then assess the view that ineffable mystical experiences could provide insight into God's nature and acts.

I

In his effort to explicate religious experience as a means for an absolutist understanding of the divine, Schleiermacher begins by focusing on "immediate self-consciousness" - i.e., awareness apart from any inferring or conscious reflection. He moves from an analysis of ordinary instances of such awareness to the (like) awareness which is the experience of God. He argues that in every ordinary instance of immediate self-consciousness there are two elements: a "feeling of freedom" - that is, a feeling of one's activity, that one can act upon and manipulate the world - and a "feeling of dependence," which is a feeling of receptivity, that there is a factor besides the self which affects oneself (6). Conjoined, these two factors give one the sense of reciprocity, of a mutual interchange with the world. Thus, I am aware of my effect on the table on which I write, the pen that I hold, and of their reciprocal effect on me.

Schleiermacher then distinguishes a third type of self-consciousness, the "feeling of absolute dependence." Whereas we can never have a feeling of absolute freedom, absolute dependence "is the consciousness that the whole of our spontaneous activity comes from a source outside of us." Schleiermacher concludes that "the whence of our receptive and active existence is implied in this self-consciousness [and] is to be designated by the word 'God'...this is for us the original signification of that word" (7). Thus, Schleiermacher identifies the experience of relation with God with the feeling of absolute dependence, and suggests that "any further content of the idea [of God] must be evolved out of this fundamental import assigned to it" (8).

There are two difficulties with Schleiermacher's procedure.

First, even if he is correct that all humans have the feeling of absolute dependence - always as a background tone or feeling, often remote and unnoticed - it does not follow that there is an objective "whence" which is the source of this feeling (and which Schleiermacher designates as "God"). Schleiermacher tends to infer the ontological fact of God's existence from the (putative) phenomenological fact of the feeling of absolute dependence. But this runs the danger of confusing phenomenology with ontology, of confusing the way things appear with the way they are. Towers at a distance may (phenomenologically) look round, but in fact be square; limbs may seem (phenomenologically) to itch, but may in fact (in cases of phantom limb) not even exist. And the experience of a fictitious, dreamt chair, may phenomenologically be exactly similar to that of a particular experience of a real chair. Feelings and sensations, however powerful and profound, whether of the mundane or the divine, are no indubitable warrant for ontological claims (though this is not to deny that the phenomenological content of our experiences is, in and of itself, evidence, and may become convincing evidence, for our knowledge of the world).

Second, Schleiermacher's procedure will not succeed in avoiding relativism, and thus he will fail to provide an absolutist understanding of God. Now he notes in The Christian Faith that his position is "intended to oppose the view that the feeling of dependence is itself conditioned by some previous knowledge about God" (9). For as he proposes earlier in On Religion, since the religious feeling (on his analysis) is pure, non-inferential and non-conceptual, it is "raised above all error and misunderstanding" (10). If one makes no inferences, uses no enculturated concepts whatsoever, and imposes none of one's own intellectual baggage of prejudice or point of view, then surely, so it would seem, one could achieve an immediate and absolute understanding of the object of one's awareness. However, a pure perceptual state of awareness is not possible.

II

During our perceptual experiences, it seems as if certain objects or states of affairs confront us and resist us, despite our best efforts to perceive them otherwise. Thus, our perceptual experiences have a certain bruteness. It is this bruteness which Schleiermacher refers to as the "feeling of dependence," expressing "the co-existence of the subject with an Other." And it might be supposed that it is precisely such brute elements in experience which constitute the "pure perceptual" components, independent of the mind's ordering, and indicative of those independent objective states of affairs which confront us and comprise "the world." Our relativized interpretations of the world are one thing; the bruteness of the world itself is quite another. As C. I. Lewis, following this line of reasoning, says about perceptual experience:

> ...there are in experience these two elements, something given and the interpretation or construction put upon it....the criteria of givenness [are]...first, its specific sensuous or feeling-character, and second, that the mode of thought can neither create nor alter it - that it remains unaffected by any change of mental attitude or interest....
> The distinction between this element of interpretation and the given is emphasized by the fact that the latter is what remains unaltered, no matter what our interests, no matter how we think or conceive. I can apprehend this thing as pen or rubber or cylinder, but I cannot by taking thought, discover it as paper or soft or cubical (11).

Insofar as the mind does order perceptual experience, let us call that ordering "conceptualization." If, with Lewis, we understand the given as "that which remains untouched and unaltered, however it is construed by thought" (12), I agree with Lewis that there is a given in perceptual experience. Now if, as Lewis suggests, the brute-fact element of any individual's perceptual experience were itself the given, then by isolating and identifying the brute-fact elements of our perceptual experiences it would be relatively easy to determine which features of perceptual experience were unconceptualized. And it might seem that we could thus determine that the feeling of absolute dependence is one such unconceptualized brute-fact element. But the given is not, as Lewis suggests, simply identical with the bruteness of our individual perceptual experiences (13).

I agree with Lewis that every perceptual experience is a construction on the given, but only as an abstraction can we distinguish the given from the mind's ordering of perceptual experience. True, were there no distinction between the given and the mind's ordering, perceptual error would be (nearly) inexplicable as long as the percipient was carefully attentive to the phenomenological content of his or her experience. But recall, for instance, Lewis's example. Given my present conceptual schema, I cannot, of course, perceive a normal writing pen as cubical or soft. But if I lacked the concept of pen or cylinder, neither could I, given that conceptual schema, perceive it as a pen or cylindrical object. As Lewis says, "'the given' [for a particular sensory stimulus] is...qualitatively no different than it would be if I were an infant or an ignorant savage" (14). But unlike the given, the brute element(s) in what an infant or an "ignorant savage" will perceive will often be different from what you or I, with our highly developed and complex Western scientific conceptual schemas, will perceive as brute. Put most generally, each brute-fact element of any individual's experience is not necessarily that which remains untouched and unaltered, however it is construed by any possible schema of thought. Hence which features of the phenomenological content of experience will possess the element of bruteness will be partially determined by conceptualization. For conceptualization is precisely what it is for our phenomenological fields to "take on" a certain look or feel (15). Consequently, if the feeling of absolute dependence is a brute element of experience, it is subject to conceptualization, and so subject to conceptual relativism.

But perhaps the feeling of absolute dependence is not a brute-fact element of experience. And in fact for Schleiermacher to suggest that the (pure) feeling of absolute dependence is not itself "conditioned by some previous [relativized] knowledge about God" is effectually for him to suggest that the feeling of absolute dependence is a given element. For brute facticity is that in each of our individual perceptual experiences which conveys the sense of unalterability; the given is that element of unalterability which must be independent of any particular experience, because it is independent of any particular percipient. Hence the given is not what any individual percipient finds is brute about his experience; the given is only what all possible percipients would discover as the common bruteness of their collective experiences. So if anything is the "pure perceptual," unconceptualized component in experience, it would be the given, and not each actual brute fact in our experience. However, identifying the feeling of absolute dependence as a given element, rather than as a mere element of brute facticity, will not resolve Schleiermacher's difficulty. For the given cannot be identified with certitude.

When we perceive what we call a writing pen, we find that just like Lewis we "cannot, by taking thought, discover it as paper or soft or cubical." But then just because I discover a (for me) unalterable brute facticity of cylindricality, or just because you and I agree about this brute facticity, that fact alone is insufficient to identify the given. At best, an individual's earnest attempt, but utter failure, to "strip away" some experiential constraint can only serve as evidence for the given; it can never serve as a criterion of the given. And from the fact that we can agree about veridical perceptions with others possessing similar conceptual schemas, all we can infer is that there is an element in our collective experiences which remains unaltered however construed by our thought: we cannot know that what is now unaltered is unalterable and so identical with the given.

In conclusion, if the feeling of absolute dependence is

given, and so unconceptualized, we could not know which brute elements of our states of self-consciousness are identical with that given. Yet if the feeling of absolute dependence is simply understood as a brute-fact element of our states of self-consciousness, we could not know that it is merely how we, with our conceptual schema(s), apprehend God. We could not know whether this feeling was just a product of our conceptualized, prior understanding of God. So whether as given, or as a mere brute element of experience, we could not know if the feeling of absolute dependence is how God confronts humans, however this event is construed by any possible schema of thought.

Setting aside then both Schleiermacher's intention to identify the feeling of absolute dependence as given (for then unapprehendable with certitude), and the notion that it is a brute-fact element of experience, consider the third alternative that the feeling of absolute dependence is itself an experience. Schleiermacher suggests that the feeling of absolute dependence is bare of human construction since "what we feel and are conscious of in religious [experience] is not the nature of things, but their operation upon us" (16). Schleiermacher is surely right about this. For instance, when I have experiences of tables and tomatoes, ships and sealing wax, I am not (ordinarily) aware of the essence of these things. I usually perceive tomatoes as things to eat, and tables as things to eat them on; not tables qua tables and tomatoes qua tomatoes. So the object of religious experience(s) is no different in this regard than the object of any of our other more common experiences. But to experience is to experience something as something. One may not even be consciously aware of the entity, X, experienced as something. Yet experiencing fundamentally involves discrimination. And to discriminate, there must be something as which the apprehended state of affairs is discriminated. Every experience, then, is conceptualized (17). And if the feeling of absolute dependence is a genuine experience, it too must be conceptualized.

Therefore, on the one hand, the very feeling of absolute dependence will be subject to the relativizing effect of the percipient's conceptual schema. For "absolute," "dependence," and even a bare "feeling" are all conceptualizations (and I do not mean that they are afterwards interpreted via concepts, though this might additionally occur). Thus Schleiermacher will fail to avoid conceptual relativism, for there will be no unconceptualized experience on which to base absolute truth-claims. It may be difficult, extremely difficult, to capture the subtle and heretofore unusual aspects of our experiences. But if we have experienced some state of affairs (call it X), then it must be possible (in principle) to articulate that experience, in however rudimentary a fashion, since that X was, necessarily, experienced as something, Y.

On the other hand, not only are experiences themselves conceptualized, but the relativistic manner in which they are (often unconsciously) conceptualized is reflected in the

Joseph Runzo

relativistic manner in which they are consciously articulated.
Schleiermacher admits that while the religious person's experience
of the Deity constitutes true piety, "to which idea [of God] he
will attach himself depends purely on what he requires it for..."
(18). We need only consider a few of the available conceptions of
the divine to see the difficulty here: Spinozan Pantheism,
Whiteheadian Pantheism, Humean Deism, and Thomist Trinitarianism
are all mutually incompatible conceptions. Now a conceptual
relativist can argue that each of these conceptions of God is true
relative to the corresponding conceptual schema(s).
Schleiermacher himself seems to accept this sort of relativism
about religions. Yet because experience itself is conceptualized,
on a Schleiermachian approach it is those very conceptualized
experiences themselves which become the principal, or at least a
major, foundation for one's explicitly articulated theological
conceptions of the divine. Thus for a position like
Schleiermacher's, which founds theology on religious experience
and attempts to avoid prior, relative notions of the divine, what
begins prima facie as the problem of the relativity of theological
conceptions, turns out to be indicative of an underlying problem
of the unavoidable relativity of primary religious experience.

III

But perhaps this conclusion is too hasty. Schleiermacher
contends that the notion of God as a distinct entity is not part
of the experience of absolute dependence per se, but one way of
expressing the import of that experience. Thus it might be argued
that it is only the attempt to reify God objectively which
involves concepts, while the actual contact or confrontation which
one has with God in the feeling of absolute dependence, or some
other genuine religious experience, is not itself conceptualized.
    Martin Buber pursues exactly this line of thought. Buber's
fundamental insight is that there is a radical difference between
relating to a thing and relating to a person in address. And
since God is a person, Buber argues that our conceptualized (and
relativized) ways of perceiving and interacting with things do not
properly apply to relating to God.
    In I and Thou Buber argues that humans have two basic
attitudes toward the world. Ontologically there is one world, but
phenomenologically there are two "worlds" - viz., the world of
experience, which he denotes with the locution "I-it," and the
world of relation, denoted by "I-thou." The "I-it" experience is
our common experience of objects in which there are two entities,
the self and the object experienced, and in which the object in
question is mediated through the manner in which it is cognized or
acted upon. Thus, the "I-it" experience involves the perception
of the object as a discrete, bounded entity, and it involves the
possibility of manipulation of the object. In contrast, the
"I-thou" relation does not (phenomenologically) involve any
objects (either the self or an other). It is an encounter, a

124

direct relationship, unmediated and void of manipulation. Where "I-it" marks an experience of something, "I-thou" marks a reciprocity, a moment of confrontation.

For Buber, though God (the Eternal Thou) is addressed and confronted in every (ordinary) "I-thou" relation, unlike other persons God can never serve as an object in an "I-it" experience (19). This leads Buber to reject Schleiermacher's notion that we can infer that God is experienced in the feeling of absolute dependence (20). On Buber's view,

> ...it is not as if God could be inferred from anything - say from nature as its cause, or from history as its helmsman, or perhaps from the subject as the self that thinks itself through it. It is not as if something else were "given" and this were then deduced from it (21).

Thus to attempt, as Schleiermacher does, to make objective statements about God as the person involved in the "I-thou" relation, is erroneously to treat an unobjectifiable thou as an "it." Human conceptualizations of God might be inherently relativistic, but on Buber's account they are inherently deficient anyway.

Buber's denial here of the possibility of natural theology - i.e., the possibility of arriving at theological truths by reason alone - and of the possibility of actually knowing God (though one can relate to God), is seriously defective. In the first place, one could not know that one was in a relationship with God unless one had some idea, however rudimentary, of the nature of God. Perhaps to countenance any conception of God is to leave oneself susceptible to the relativity of all enculturated thought. But be that as it may, to attempt (implicitly) to identify God merely as "that in which I am in relation in the 'I-thou' relation with the Eternal Thou" is vacuously tautological.

In the second place, Buber's position is self-stultifying. In saying that God cannot be treated as an it, Buber himself treats God as an it:

> By its very nature the eternal You cannot become an It; because by its very nature it cannot be placed within measure and limit, not even within the measure of the immeasurable and the limit of the unlimited; because of its very nature it cannot be grasped as a sum of qualities that have been raised to transcendence....(22).

What warrant could Buber have for this claim (excluding direct divine revelation, a view which I will assess shortly)? There are two possibilities. This view of the nature of God might be a presupposition in metaphysics. But then we need not accept it without further argument. And even if we do accept it as a thesis in metaphysics, it quite clearly employs concepts (in Buber's terminology, it is within the "I-it" realm).

Or, this view of the nature of God might be (despite Buber's denial) an inferential conclusion from the phenomenology of the "I-Thou" relation. In that case, either Buber supposes that what appears to be the case must be the case, thus confusing phenomenology with ontology, or he is depending on what is at best a weak inference from phenomenological facts to propositions about reality. And in the latter instance, Schleiermacher could for example counter that he has made the same sort of inferential judgment, except that Schleiermacher concludes that we can properly say that God possesses certain infinite attributes. But in any event, Buber has again provided a conception of the nature of God which will be as subject to the relativizing effect of enculturated perceptions, concepts, inclinations, etc., as is any other conception.

However, though Buber's position thus fails to escape the problem of conceptual relativism, it raises two issues which remain to be addressed. First, might a direct revelation from God during a mystical vision avoid the problem of relativism? Second, Buber holds that the "I-Thou" relation with the Eternal Thou is ineffable - that it is unconceptualizable, though it provides insight. Could ineffable mystical experiences provide an absolute insight into the nature of God?

IV

Focusing first on mystical visions, could a mystical vision provide an absolute insight into the divine, which avoids the relativity of human conception? As a first step, it should be noted that in the mystic literature there are two uses of "vision." "Vision" can be used (a) to denote an experience, where the recipient can be referred to as having the vision, or (b) to denote an object, where the recipient can be referred to as perceiving the vision - i.e., there is an external state of affairs, the vision, of which the percipient becomes aware. I will refer to the two types of visions as "received visions" and "perceived visions," respectively (23).

During received visions there is no perceived object the details of which the percipient can scan or otherwise focus his or her attention on to the exclusion of other, concurrent details of the vision. The vision is the percipient's experience. In contradistinction to received visions, numerous visionary objects are only seen if the percipient looks in the correct physical place at the right time, and many visions are publicly observable states of affairs. In both cases, the visions will be perceived visions, the vision being an external state of affairs which the percipient perceives. Even more strongly, the externality of the perceived state of affairs in perceived visions is indicated by the percipient's ability to scan the vision visually. To take an example, Julian of Norwich implies that as she gazed at an actual crucifix held before her, she had a vision which was an object, the details of which she could look at: "the bleeding [of Christ] continued and could be seen by attentive eyes....I knew that while I gazed on the cross I was safe and sound" (24).

Let us examine perceived visions first. Suppose that a mystic purports to perceive God by means of sensory perceptions, or to hear God speak through auditory "mystical locutions," during a vision. Could God thus directly reveal Himself, or truths about Himself, and so enable the mystic to circumvent enculturated and relativistic patterns of thought and perception?

Clearly, to the extent that mystical visions involve genuine sense perception, to that extent they will be subject to the same epistemic strictures as ordinary sense perception. And just as ordinary sense perception is thoroughly conceptualized, the phenomenological content of perceived visions will be thoroughly conceptualized. As already noted, a genuine act of perception minimally involves the discrimination of a discrete "something," X. Now, this might involve the differentiation of the perceived entity, X, from its environmental field, or as is shown by the case of perceiving only a uniform surface, this discrimination might not involve the specific differentiation of X from a background. Yet whether or not one is aware of other entities composing a definite and contrasting environmental field, some X is discriminated. And to discriminate X is to discriminate X as something - however indefinite or amorphous. Hence to perceive X is to perceive X as something. However, to perceive as is to categorize (even if unconsciously and unreflectively) (25). And this applies to perceived visions.

Isaiah (of Jerusalem) records a perceived mystical vision as follows:

> In the year that King Uzziah died I saw the
> Lord sitting upon a throne, high and lifted
> up; and his train filled the temple. Above
> him stood the seraphim; each had six wings...
> And one called to another and said:
>   "Holy, holy holy is the Lord of hosts;
>   the whole earth is full of his glory."
> ...And I said: "Woe is me!...for my eyes have
> seen the King, the Lord of hosts!" (Isaiah
> 6:1-3, 5 [R.S.V.])

In this vision, Isaiah discriminates the central visionary object from a background of seraphim, the surrounding temple, etc. And Isaiah discriminates that visionary object as something - viz., as a man-like figure, as enthroned, as uttering words to him (Isaiah 6:6-13). These are all conceptualizations. That is, in the account, Isaiah (perhaps unconsciously) perceives God in terms of the categories of thought and belief which he already possesses:

king, enthroned, and so on. Without these concepts, Isaiah could not have had the experience which he did, for then he would not have been able to see God as king, as enthroned. For since there are no "pure perceptual experiences" apart from the mind's ordering, the possession of concepts is a necessary condition of all perceptual experience. For, once again, to perceive is to perceive as, and to perceive something as X the percipient must possess the appropriate conceptual resources to understand Xness (26).

Against this "conceptualist position," that the possession of concepts is a necessary condition for perceptual experience, Fred Dretske has argued "what makes our visual experience the rich and profuse thing we know it to be is that we see more than we ever notice or attend to" (27). The same sort of point could be raised regarding the mystic's perceived vision: surely the richness of the mystical experience is not to be limited to whatever the mystic might tell us about his or her experience. But all this shows is that our (conceptualized) unreflective perceptual experience is far richer than our (conceptualized) reflective perceptual experience. The mystic may never be reflectively aware of numerous conceptualized elements which he or she unreflectively perceives.

Further, in supporting his own anti-conceptualist view, Dretske inadvertently brings out the total conceptualization of perceptual experience by comparing our sensory system to a postal system. He says that the sensory system:

> ...is responsible for the delivery of information, and its responsibility ends there. What we do with this information, once received, whether we are even capable of interpreting the messages so received, are questions about the cognitive-conceptual resources of the perceiver. If you don't take the letters from the mailbox, or if you don't understand them once you do, don't blame the postal system (28).

This talk of "information" and "messages" is systematically conceptualization-laden. Nerve impulses (or for that matter, phosphenes) are no more bits of information than are irruptions on a magnetic tape or the rings in the trunk of a tree. In and of themselves, these are all just physical states of affairs. Information has to do with how such states of affairs are understood, or understandable. One man's message is another man's puff of smoke. Tree rings and magnetic tapes only become informative when the informee takes their physical configurations to be indicative of something. Genuine information is information about something, information of some conceptual type; genuine information is propositional.

I have no quarrel with the basic perception-as-postal-system metaphor. As Dretske says, "To say that someone has seen X is to say that information about X has been delivered in a particular form..." (29). Putting this in conceptualist terms, our non-inferential visual information about some X is of the conceptualized form seen as Y. But then, perception, and the perceptual aspects of perceived visions, are fundamentally information-bearing, and hence are radically conceptualized.

The only way to avoid this conclusion is to suppose that there can be theory-neutral, or category-neutral, perceptual "information." That supposition not only, as just suggested, rests on a misunderstanding of the nature of information; it assumes that there is available to us some concept-neutral "stuff" about which perceptual experience is informative. But that reverts to the suggestion that there are "pure," potentially knowable components to perceptual experience. And I have already argued that, except for the unknowable given, there are no pure, unconceptualized elements in experience. The brute facticity of our perceptual experiences, whether I am viewing a writing pen or having a (perceived) vision of God, is the bruteness of my experience, mediated via my conceptual schema. The mystic cannot know that what appears unalterable in his or her visionary experience is ultimately unalterable - that is, would be so perceived by any percipient no matter what the conceptual structure of his or her conceptual schema(s). Hence perceived visions could not provide an absolute, unconceptualized insight into the nature or acts of God which avoids conceptual relativism.

Still, if the phenomenological content of perceptual experience is inextricably wedded to the conceptual structure of the percipient's conceptual schema, it might be supposed that it is by means of received visions instead that the mystic could evade the relativizing effect of one's conceptual schema. For received visions do not involve literal sense perceptions, though (usually) they are transmitted in terms of sensory images (30). Unfortunately there are two related difficulties with this proposal.

The first difficulty is a general one affecting the epistemic reliability of any type of vision, but I will consider it now vis-a-vis received visions. Mystics themselves are frequently apprehensive about whether their visions are veridical. Within the Christian mystical tradition there have been two traditional tests of veridicality. Nelson Pike has identified the first as the "spiritual-effects test" (31). This is the principle that visions which are indeed produced by God result in positive spiritual effects, such as feelings of joy, love, and quietude, and are conducive to a spiritual life, one of humility, moral rectitude, etc. The second test, which Pike refers to as the "Scripture-dogma test," is the principle representatively enunciated as follows by St. Teresa of Avila:

> ...as far as I can see and learn by
> experience, the soul must be convinced that a

> thing comes from God only if it is in
> conformity with Holy Scripture; if it were to
> diverge from that in the least, I think I
> should be incomparably more firmly convinced
> that it came from the devil than I previously
> was that it came from God, however sure I
> might have felt of this (32).

Working with Pike's distinctions, George Mavrodes offers an insightful analysis of the ultimate hopelessness of attempts like Teresa's to give criteria for the veridicality of visions (33). As Mavrodes points out, precisely the same sort of difficulties, e.g., deception by the devil, which concern Teresa, would affect the "Scripture-dogma" and "spiritual effects" tests, as would affect the original purported content of the vision in question. For once doubt about the origin and hence the veridicality of a vision has been raised, it is of course possible that a non-veridical vision be attended by positive spiritual side-effects, and possible that the content of a particular vision nowhere contradicts the already articulated orthodox doctrine, though it in fact contains elements which would be, let us say, considered heretical were they assessed theologically (for the first time).

Now let us apply Mavrodes's general point to our present concern. Suppose the "Scripture-dogma" and "spiritual effects" tests were used to test for the absoluteness of the truth conveyed by a vision. Unfortunately, any doubt about the absoluteness of the truth conveyed by a vision will equally apply to the correctness of application of these second-order criteria of veridicality. For visions conveying merely relative truths could produce positive spiritual effects and could accord with articulated orthodox doctrine. Hence any feeling of surety about the truth of either of these two criteria for the veridicality of visions, or about the correctness of their application in a particular instance, is just as open to doubt as the original sense of surety that one's vision has a divine origin and that it conveys absolute truths about God.

The second difficulty with received visions is simply this. Even if God is their author (and the human recipient is not actively involved in the production of the vision), a received vision cannot convey knowledge of God unless the putative knowledge can (in principle) be rendered in propositions by the recipient(s). And however the epistemic import of a received vision is propositionalized, some schema or other of concepts must be used. Clearly, if the concepts employed are humanly understandable, then if one is concerned about the relativity of human conception, the resultant truth-claims will still be subject to a relative, human perspective, insight, habits of thought, etc. So if conceptual relativism is acknowledged, either received visions convey no knowledge, or they (necessarily) convey only conceptual-schema-relative truths, and, in this sense, they cannot provide absolute insight (34).

V

We saw earlier that Martin Buber holds that the "I-Thou" relation with God cannot properly be described. God, says Buber, is "not even within the measure of the immeasurable and the limit of the unlimited." Putting aside the problem of self-stultification in this claim that God cannot be described because he has certain (nameable) qualities, let us now turn to the claim that ineffable mystical experiences could provide an absolute insight into the divine. When we articulate our experiences, we must articulate them in terms of our conceptual schemas; but if there are elements of our experience (or relationships) which are inherently inexpressible, might not that very ineffability remove those elements of our experience from the tincture of the relativity of our ordinary, enculturated, conceptualizations? What is unconceptualizable obviously cannot be subject to the relativity of conceptualization.

The answer to this question will depend on what is meant by "ineffability." In one use of "ineffability," the experience is understandable to the participant, yet since the experience is so unlike other sorts of experience, it cannot be adequately explained, and certainly not defined, to those who have not themselves had the experience (35). But this is no different than numerous instances of ordinary experience. Thus the taste of milk and the experience of seeing red are experiences of this sort, not fully expressible to those who have not had the relevant experience. The sighted and gustatorily endowed understand "the seeing of red" and "the taste of milk," for in order to have these perceptual experiences they must possess such concepts as "red," "milk," "seeing," and so forth. Similarly, if the non-religious can come to have and understand the experience of the mystic, then they too will understand the relevant concepts. In this sense of "ineffability," the percipient's own conceptual schema still ultimately provides the possibility for understanding the experience.

A quite different sort of ineffability of mystical experiences is proposed by Walter Stace. Stace suggests that for both Eastern and Western mystical experiences of the Godhead or of Brahman, "no concepts apply to them" (36). This is related to the kind of "pure" mystical experience which Aldous Huxley writes about in The Doors of Perception and Heaven and Hell, his fascinating accounts of his experiences under the influence of mescalin. Huxley argues that the "medium of concepts...distorts every given fact into the all too familiar likeness of some generic label or explanatory abstraction" (37). And he evocatively suggests that, much like traditional mystical experiences, concepts are bypassed during the mescalin experience and "the doors of perception [are] cleansed," "everything [appearing] to man as it is" (William Blake):

131

> That chair - shall I ever forget it? Where
> the shadows fell on the canvas upholstery,
> stripes of a deep but glowing indigo
> alternated with stripes of incandescence so
> intensely bright that it was hard to believe
> that they could be made of anything but blue
> fire....Today the percept had swallowed up the
> concept....Garden furniture, lathes, sunlight,
> shadow - these were no more than names and
> notions, mere verbalizations, for utilitarian
> or scientific purposes, after the event. The
> event was this succession of azure furnace
> doors separated by gulfs of unfathomable
> gentian (38).

Thus on Huxley's account, except for utilitarian and scientific
purposes after the experience, concepts are not directly
applicable to the experience. Anything ineffable in this strong
sense of Stace's and Huxley's, anything to which no concepts
apply, could not be subject to conceptual relativism. Perhaps
then, strongly ineffable, unconceptualizable mystical experiences
could provide an absolute insight into the nature and acts of God.
Stace bases his formulation of "ineffable," that "no concepts
apply," in part on the assumption that the experience of the
Godhead (or of Brahman) must remain utterly ineffable to the
mystic herself or himself: "...the mystic himself...finds his
vision ineffable and unutterable. It is he who experiences the
difficulty, not we" (39). The great thirteenth-century German
mystic, Meister Eckhart, holds that "the onefold One has neither a
manner nor properties." This would seem to support Stace's view
of strong ineffability. But Eckhart means by this that one must
give up all usual conceptions of God. In mystical union it is
necessary for God to enter the soul apart from "all his [commonly
attributed] divine names and personlike properties" (40). It is
in this sense of the inapplicability of ordinary concepts that for
Eckhart knowledge of the Godhead cannot be communicated.
It is crucial to recognize that the mystic cannot
meaningfully (semantically) use such locutions as "the Godhead" if
they have absolutely no conceptual content. Otherwise, a sentence
like "The Godhead is One" would have no more meaning than "____ is
One." And in fact for Eckhart "the Godhead" does not function
syntactically as a mere place holder. "The Godhead is not lower
than God" is a truth for Eckhart. Thus the "mystic ascent" is a
path of knowledge for Eckhart, though he distinguishes it as a
different kind of knowledge from common forms of knowledge.
For Eckhart a conflict arises between talk about mystic union
with the Godhead, on the one hand, and the more ordinary theistic
language of Eckhart's contemporaries, on the other. Eckhart holds
that

> ...the soul enters the unity of the Holy

Trinity but it may become even more blessed by
going further, to the barren Godhead, of which
the Trinity is a revelation (41).

On the more accepted conception of his contemporaries, the triune
God is the ultimate ontological reality; on Eckhart's view, the
Godhead is that ultimate ontological reality. And whereas God is
identifiable by His attributes, the Godhead - the ultimate goal,
for Eckhart, of the mystic path - is "without activity or form."
    In essence, a conflict has thus arisen between two
incompatible conceptual schemas. It is not that no concepts apply
to the experience (Stace), or that "the percept has swallowed up
the concept" (Huxley). Rather, the conceptual schema appropriate
to Eckhart's mystical experiences contradicts portions of the
conceptual schema of traditional Christian trinitarianism. This
conflict becomes expressed as the claim that the mystical
experience is "ineffable" - i.e., inexpressible in ordinary
religious language with its underlying trinitarian conceptual
schema (42). But the mystic who, like Eckhart, claims that his or
her experience is a knowledge context, is employing some
conceptual schema. Even if the concept of the Godhead is a
primitive - and hence can only be communicated via ostension - the
mystic presumably understands the concept. And once again if ex
hypothesi conceptual relativism is accepted, the fact that
mystical experiences are ineffable in the sense of not being
communicable vis-a-vis ordinary language still leaves the
epistemic content of the experience subject to relativism.

VI

    One last defense of the putative absolute insight which could
be provided by ineffable mystical experiences might yet be raised
at this juncture. We have seen that the ineffability of mystical
experiences can in some cases be explained in terms of a conflict
of conceptual schemas, between the mystic's talk about the
Godhead, on the one hand, and ordinary religious conceptual
schema(s), on the other. Now it might be supposed, as is
frequently claimed, that mystical understanding need not be
amenable to the laws of (human) logic. Hence it might be argued
that the relativity of those "merely" human laws need not affect
the epistemic import of the genuine mystical experience.
Ordinarily it might be contradictory to claim that one has
non-propositional, unconceptualizable knowledge. But niceties of
logic and considerations of consistency do not, so it is sometimes
suggested, apply to genuine mystical experiences.
    For example, in Mysticism East and West, Rudolph Otto states
that there is a "peculiar logic of mysticism," which discounts the
two fundamental laws of natural logic: the law of Contradiction
and of the Excluded Third" (43). And Eliot Deutsch argues in
Advaita Vedanta that "logic is grounded in the mind as it relates
to the phenomenal order; hence, it is unable to affirm, without at

the same time denying, what extends beyond that order" (44). But these are self-refuting positions.

To use language to claim that the law of non-contradiction does not apply in some instance is self-contradictory and defeats the purpose of that very use of language. If the law of non-contradiction does not hold universally, then it does not hold at all, for it is a universal metalogical claim about all propositions. And if the law of non-contradiction does not hold, then the claim that it sometimes does not hold is itself no more true than it is false. Furthermore, it would be unintelligible to use allegedly rational discourse, dependent on the law of non-contradiction, to argue that the proposition expressed by the law of non-contradiction might be false. This proposal could not even be framed, and would always fall into sheer nonsense, since an argument is only valid when, if the premises are true, the conclusion could not be false.

Lastly, the truth of the law of non-contradiction is essential to the intelligibility of any statement, since any statement is only intelligible on the assumption that its negation is not concomitantly true also. As Aristotle observed in the Metaphysics about this "most indisputable of all principles":

> We can...demonstrate...that this view [the denial of the law of non-contradiction] is impossible, if our opponent will only say something...which is significant both for himself and for another; for this is necessary if he really is to say anything. For, if he means nothing, such a man will not be capable of reasoning, either with himself or with another (45).

A language game can only be meaningfully used as long as one consistently adheres to the logic of that language game given the meaning rules of that language game and the law of non-contradiction (46). Thus to the extent that mystics aspire to communicate anything semantically meaningful to non-mystics, mystics must be logically consistent. It is simply nonsense to claim that they employ a "logic" of their own which excludes the law of non-contradiction. And to claim otherwise opens one to Ambrose Bierce's apt satirization of the nonsensical appeal to incomprehensibility which has all too often been religion's disreputable stigma:

> In religion we believe only what we do not understand, except in the instance of an intelligible doctrine that contradicts an incomprehensible one. In that case we believe the former as a part of the latter (Bierce, "Trinity," in Devil's Dictionary).

In short, for mystics like Eckhart who regard their experiences as providing a _knowledge_ of God, whatever knowledge is acquired must be consistently propositionalizable in terms of _some_ conceptual schema. And whatever conceptual schema, however extraordinary, is employed, if a _human_ understanding has been achieved, it will _ipso facto_ be a _humanly_ conditioned conceptual schema. But that is to say that however the experience might be otherwise ineffable, any _knowledge_ gained through the mystical experience will be as subject to conceptual relativism as are more ordinary forms of knowledge. Consequently, mystical experiences can offer no unconceptualized, absolute insight into God's nature and actions (47). And if the mystic still insists that the experience is _utterly_ ineffable, and so not subject to the vicissitudes of the relativity of our human conceptual schemas, then as William Alston has observed:

> To label something ineffable in an unqualified
> way is to shirk the job of making explicit the
> ways in which it _can_ be talked about;...there
> may be something _in_ the world which can't be
> talked about in any way, but if so we can only
> signalize the fact by leaving it unrecorded
> (48).

VII

Paul Holmer has recently argued that "theological language has a definitive role, which is to intensify and to purify religious passion" (49). Yet however rightfully prominent the passional element in theology and faith, there must be a propositional element in theology and faith. For notwithstanding Schleiermacher's observation that "Quantity of knowledge is not quantity of piety" (50), piety without propositional content is contentless passion. Hence the retreat into the supposed ineffability of the religious experience is pointless if it is viewed as a means of giving substance to religion and of avoiding the relativity of human conception.

It is perhaps appropriate that one philosopher who saw this clearly was David Hume. In the _Dialogues_ _Concerning_ _Natural_ _Religion_, Hume has Cleanthes say:

> The Deity, I can readily allow, possesses many
> powers and attributes of which we can have no
> comprehension; but if our ideas, so far as
> they go, be not just and adequate and
> correspondent to his real nature, I know not
> what there is in this subject worth insisting
> on. Is the name, without any meaning, of such
> mighty importance? Or how do you _mystics_, who
> maintain the absolute incomprehensibility of
> the Deity, differ from sceptics or atheists,

Joseph Runzo

who assert that the first cause of all is
unknown and unintelligible? (51)

On the one hand we have seen that the notion of a comprehensible
but "pure," unconceptualized religious experience is specious.
Yet on the other hand, I agree with Hume that those who
fundamentally appeal to the utter ineffability of religious
experience are "atheists without knowing it." Therefore, one must
look elsewhere than to religious experience simpliciter in order
to address the challenge of conceptual relativism. For if one
hopes to find a means whereby the substantive content of theology
and faith can be (in some sense) absolute and not, in Karl Barth's
words, "accursedly relative" (52), we must recognize that
religious experience in itself offers no such hope (53).

NOTES

1. Paul Tillich, Systematic Theology (Chicago: University of
Chicago Press, 1951), Vol. 1, p. 3.

2. H. Richard Niebuhr, Christ and Culture (New York: Harper and
Row, Harper Torchbooks, 1951), p. 238.

3. More precisely, conceptual relativism is restricted to object
language truths. Conceptual relativism alone exempts, e.g.,
metalogical principles from relativism. A rather different sort
of relativism, what we might call "epistemological relativism,"
would concern the relativity of metalogical principles, criteria
for coming to know something, criteria for semantic meaning, and
the like. Epistemological relativism will not be addressed in
this paper.

4. Friedrich Schleiermacher, On Religion: Speeches to its
Cultured Despisers (New York: Harper and Row, 1958), p. 13. For
Schleiermacher's view that theology is subject to relativism, see
p. 50.

5. I offer an analysis of how a conceptual relativist account of
theistic truth-claims might be defended in "Religion, Relativism,
and Conceptual Schemas," The Heythrop Journal, Vol. 23, No. 1
(Jan. 1983).

6. Friedrich Schleiermacher, The Christian Faith (Edinburgh: T.
and T. Clark, 1928), pp. 13-14.

7. Ibid., p. 16.

8. Ibid., p. 17. Schleiermacher essentially attempts to generate

136

a systematic theology out of the character of basic religious experience. (See also p. 10.)

9. Ibid., p. 17.

10. Schleiermacher, On Religion, p. 43.

11. C. I. Lewis, Mind and the World Order (New York: Dover Publications, 1956), pp. 48, 52, and 66.

12. Ibid., p. 55.

13. Ibid., p. 57.

14. Ibid., p. 50.

15. It is this unmanipulable bruteness which conveys that sense of something being "presented" that, in part, distinguishes perceiving from imagining phenomenologically. And we cannot manipulate these elements because the referents of this partially mind-imposed bruteness are states of affairs which are categorized, given our conceptual schemas, as possible actual states of affairs.

16. Schleiermacher, On Religion, p. 48.

17. Kant perspicuously puts this point in his famous dictum about sense perception: "...[sensible] intuitions without concepts are blind." Immanuel Kant, Critique of Pure Reason, trans. Norman Kemp Smith (England: Macmillan, 1929), p. 93.

18. Schleiermacher, On Religion, p. 98. One parallel in the twentieth century to Schleiermacher's position is John Baillie's notion that all people have a direct experience of God and that

> In working out our conviction that all men believe in God, we have now come to see that they may nevertheless believe in Him in very different ways. In particular, we have found ourselves distinguishing two ways of believing which fall short of the full Christian way. There is the man who has never doubted that God is, but who lives as though He were not; and there is the man who doubts whether God is, or even denies He is, but lives as though He were. (Our Knowledge of God [New York: Scribner's, 1959], p. 75.)

19. Martin Buber, I and Thou, trans. Walter Kaufmann (New York: Scribner's, 1970), p. 147.

20. Besides the reason noted, two other reasons which Buber explicitly offers are that (1) in referring to the religious experience as a "self-consciousness," there is an overemphasis on the self, and (2) feelings "merely accompany the fact of the relationship," and since feelings are quantifiable, to speak about one's feelings is to treat something as an object which one can respond to and manipulate.

21. Buber, I and Thou, p. 129.

22. Ibid., p. 160.

23. This terminology, and the following discussion, are taken from my "Visions, Pictures, and Rules," Religious Studies, Vol. 13 (Sept. 1977), pp. 303-318. (Reprinted by permission of Cambridge University Press.)

24. Julian of Norwich, Revelations of Divine Love, trans. Clifton Wolters (Baltimore: Penguin Books, 1966), Chs. 12 and 19.

25. Cf. George Pitcher, A Theory of Perception (Princeton: Princeton University Press, 1971), p. 94: "The way things look (even in the phenomenal sense) to a perceiver is partially dependent on what his repertoire of concepts is..." Conceptualists like Pitcher and D. M. Armstrong hold that perceptual acts are definitively either acquisitions of beliefs or inclinations to believe. While I agree about the necessity of concepts for perception, I think that a perceptual act is not definitively explicable in terms of beliefs but, more fundamentally, consists in an episodically occurrent awareness of propositions about states of affairs of the percipient's body and environment. Thus, percieving X as Y does not necessarily involve the acquisition of beliefs about X - or Y. (See my "The Propositional Structure of Perception," American Philosophical Quarterly, Vol. 14, No. 3 [July 1977], pp. 219-20.)

26. I defend this conceptualist position in greater detail in "The Radical Conceptualization of Perceptual Experience," American Philosophical Quarterly, Vol. 19, No. 3 (July 1982), pp. 205-217, from which several arguments in this paper were drawn. (Reprinted by permission of the Editor.)

27. Fred Dretske, "Simple Seeing," in Body, Mind and Method, eds. D. Gustafson and B. Tapscott (Boston: D. Reidel, 1979), p. 3.

28. Ibid., pp. 10-11.

29. Ibid., p. 10.

30. Beginning with Augustine (see A Literal Commentary on Genesis, Book 12), visions have traditionally been divided in the

Christian mystical tradition into three categories: "corporeal" visions, which involve the use of the bodily senses; "imaginary" visions, which do not involve the literal use of the bodily senses but phenomenologically involve sensory images; and "intellectual" visions, which are usually regarded as not involving either the bodily senses or sensory imagery. The present point, then, applies to received, "imaginary" visions (and possibly to received "intellectual" visions).

31. Nelson Pike, "On Mystic Visions as Sources of Knowledge," in *Mysticism and Philosophical Analysis*, ed. Stephen T. Katz (New York: Oxford University Press, 1979), pp. 214-234.

32. St. Teresa of Avila, *The Autobiography of St. Teresa of Avila*, trans. E. Allison Peers, Ch. 25, p. 239.

33. George Mavrodes, "Real vs. Deceptive Mystical Visions," in *Mysticism and Philosophical Analysis*, p. 251.

34. For an extended analysis of how it *is possible* for mystics to identify the figures in visions, see my "Visions, Pictures, and Rules."

35. For instance, Rudolf Otto suggests that the experience of the "numenous" is

> ...sui *generis* and irreducible to any other; and therefore, like every absolutely primary and elementary datum, while it admits of being discussed, it cannot be strictly defined...[This experience] cannot, strictly speaking, be taught, it can only be evoked, awakened in the mind...(Otto, *The Idea of the Holy* [London: Oxford University Press, 1923], p. 7).

36. Walter Stace, *Time and Eternity* (Princeton, N.J.: Princeton University Press, 1952, p. 33 (italics mine).

37. Aldous Huxley, *The Doors of Perception* (New York: Harper and Row, 1954), p. 74.

38. Ibid., pp. 53-54.

39. Walter Stace, *Time and Eternity*, p. 39.

40. Eckhart, Sermon on Lk. 10:38, in *Meister Eckhart*, trans. Raymond B. Blakney (New York: Harper Torchbooks, 1941), p. 211. (See also Eckhart's sermon on Lk. 2:42, in *Meister Eckhart*, pp. 118-119.)

41. Eckhart, Sermon on John 16:7, ibid., p. 200.

42. Moreover, the fact that the ineffability of the experience of the Godhead results from a difference of conceptual schemas indicates why the via negativa is not, as is often supposed, an effective means of apprehending an absolutist epistemic import for mystical experiences. Eckhart, like many other mystics, makes some use of the via negativa: "God is neither being nor goodness...God is neither good, better or best." (Sermon on Ecclesiasticus 50:6-7, in Meister Eckhart, p. 220.) Yet the via negativa is of no avail here because it would incorrectly presuppose that the mystic, who has the experience of the Godhead, and the non-mystic, who is striving for that experience, would be speaking from within the conceptual strictures of the same conceptual schema.

43. Rudolf Otto, Mysticism East and West (New York: MacMillan, 1932), p. 64.

44. Eliot Deutsch, Advaita Vedanta (Hawaii: University of Hawaii Press, 1971), p. 11.

45. Aristotle, Metaphysics, in The Basic Works of Aristotle (New York, 1941), 10069, 12-15.

46. Thus even the object language relativism of conceptual relativism depends for its coherence on accepting the metalogical principle of non-contradiction as an absolute, trans-schema truth.

47. The conclusion that mystical experiences cannot open some non-relativistic "doors of perception" to absolute truths about God should not be so surprising, however, when it is recognized that at least in the Christian tradition, mystics have not in fact usually claimed a greater knowledge of the divine through their experience. Thus St. Teresa holds that it is good works which are the primary fruit of Spiritual Marriage:

> ...finding ways to please [Christ]...This, my daughters, is the aim of prayer: this is the purpose of the Spiritual Marriage, of which are born good works and good works alone.
> Such works, as I have told you, are the sign of every genuine favour and of everything else that comes from God. (Interior Castle [Garden City, N.Y.: Image, 1961], trans. E. Allison Peers, p. 228.)

And Teresa concludes her Interior Castle with an admonition to place the mystic way in its proper perspective:

> ...let none of you imagine that, because a

sister has had such experiences, she is any
better than the rest; the Lord leads each of
us as He sees we have need. Such experiences,
if we use them aright, prepare us to be better
servants of God (Interior Castle, p. 184).

48. William Alston, "Ineffability," in Philosophy of Religion,
ed. Steven M. Cahn (New York: Harper and Row, 1970), pp. 299-300.

49. Paul Holmer, The Grammar of Faith (San Francisco: Harper and
Row, 1978), p. 67.

50. Schleiermacher, On Religion, p. 35.

51. David Hume, Dialogues Concerning Natural Religion, ed. Nelson
Pike (Indianapolis: Bobbs-Merrill, 1970), p. 40.

52. Karl Barth, The Epistle to the Romans (Oxford: Oxford
University Press, 1968), p. 255.

53. I am indebted to Stephen T. Davis, John Hick, Gregory Kavka,
Mike W. Martin, and Philip L. Quinn for their helpful comments on
an earlier version of this paper, and to the National Endowment
for the Humanities for a Fellowship for College Teachers under
which I wrote this paper.

(Much of this article appears as Chapter 3 in my book,
Reason, Relativism, and God (London: The Macmillan Press,
Ltd., 1985; New York: St. Martin's Press, 1986) and is
reprinted here by permission of The Macmillan Press, Ltd.
and St. Martin's Press.)